This book is for Everett and Mimi Simson and the St. Luke's family.

"There is much else that Jesus did. If it were all to be recorded in detail, I suppose the whole world could not hold the books that would be written."

(John 21:25, NEB)

1

The young man yawned and stretched.

"You are restless?" Miriam asked her lover.

Reuven shrugged. "Nothing ever happens here in Cana." Then, almost maliciously, he grinned. "There's a cure for such restlessness."

Miriam's left eyebrow lifted. "Yes. And the physician is with you."

He laughed, springing up from the mat on which he lay. He embraced her and then he said, "You know the gown I like best? The blue one from Egypt?"

"I know." She stroked his cheek. "Of course I know."

"Please put it on. And use the Egyptian cosmetics to enlarge your mysterious amber eyes. And twine the gold and lapis in your hair. Oh Miriam, I love your hair. I wish I could name it. It is not gold. It is not red. It is like sun on metal."

"How poetic you are." Miriam's tone was indulgent. "And where are we going, that I should dress so lavishly in the middle of the day?"

"I will tell you when you are dressed."

"Tell me now," she coaxed.

"No. Later. Hurry, Miriam. I wish I had thought of it sooner."

When Miriam was ready she stood before him in the gown she had brought with her from Egypt. It was the color of her lapis lazuli rings and necklace.

He stared at her. "I never get used to it," he said. "You are too beautiful." He took her face between his hands. "But I can never reach you completely. You hide from me. What is it you hide?"

She could not hide her beauty. At forty she had the fresh look of youth, an exotic matte pallor of skin. Childless, she had the body of a girl. Despite the excesses and depravities of her life, she remained lovely.

She laid her own right hand against his in a practiced gesture. Her hand was warm. Although her inner self was cold as stone, she knew that no man could guess her heart. To men she seemed all fire. Her secret was too deep to be perceived. She smiled at him and asked, "Now tell me, Reuven. Where are we going?"

"It is the fifth day of my friend's wedding festivities," he said. "I'm going to take you there."

She paused before she asked him, "Do you think that is wise?"

Again he shrugged. "They all talk anyway. Everyone here in Cana knows who you are. Who we are. What difference will it make? You will be the most beautiful woman there. Let them talk. No one will throw stones."

Miriam shuddered. Stonings were no small matter, and she was vulnerable. Stonings led to death . . . slow, painful death. "Think about it for a moment, my love," she said to the man who was so much younger than herself. "You do not want your friend to be upset on this auspicious occasion." Her tone was ironic, but she was only half joking.

"Come." He led her out. Walking along the narrow streets toward the house of his friend, they heard the merriment before they reached it: laughter, singing, and the sounds of pipe, drums, and cymbals.

Outside the house tables were placed under shelters made of palm fronds. Children chased each other, dogs barked, the scent of roasting meat rose on the still air. The tall ablution vessels stood near the door.

Miriam's lover pulled her inside with him. "Shall I present you to the parents of my friend, the bridegroom?" He teased her without malice.

"You are an idiot," she answered, also without malice.

For a moment a palpable silence filled the room as people stared at Miriam. But soon the singing resumed. Her lover led her to a mat where a group of young men sat drinking wine. They looked up at her. Haughty as a princess she stared down at them. She could read their faces. There was not one among them who did not desire her. Young men drifted to Miriam as moths to flame. They knew that she could teach them things they never dreamed of. They also knew that only the wealthy could afford her company. And their friend was wealthy. But they did not know her secret. She despised them all.

"Sit with us, Reuven," one of the young men said, "so that we too may enjoy your companion's beauty."

As easily as if she were a girl instead of a woman of forty years, Miriam sank to the floor, her blue gown flowing around her.

She glanced about, meeting looks of scorn with bold challenge. She saw the young bride dressed in white, a fringe of gold coins at her forehead, daisies and marigolds wreathed about her headdress.

The poor little fool, Miriam thought. *She thinks she is about to step into a bright new life.* Miriam fleetingly remembered her mother, the many painful birthings, the harsh poverty. And her mother's eternal bitterness.

Taking a goblet of wine from her lover, she sipped it. He whispered to her, "That's the host, my friend's father." Miriam glanced toward the place where the bride and bridegroom sat near their parents. She noticed a man who was seated near the host.

He looked tall and slender, perhaps a bit too slender. His body appeared disciplined, lean, and virile. Miriam had come to value a well-built body. Too many men were gross and slovenly. This man's hair fell thick and smooth along his shoulders. His beard was neat. He was simply dressed in a seamless, homespun robe. *There,* she thought, *is a man I could almost desire.*

As if he felt Miriam's eyes upon him, he looked across at her. She smiled at him, the warmest smile she could summon. She knew that her smiles were said to ignite all that was flammable in a man.

But this man did not return her smile. He looked at her with a gaze so straight and clear that for a moment she thought she had seen it before. It was a stern look, but calm, forgiving. There was grief in it, too. He looked at her as if he grieved on her account.

Confused, Miriam looked away. She wanted to feel anger at this man who ignored her smile. But she felt only confusion. So she looked away from him toward the woman who sat beside him, wondering what kind of a woman would please him.

As Miriam studied the woman's face, her own face became warm. Her heart began a crazy pattern of beats which she thought might suffocate her. The palms of her hands grew moist and she wanted to run away. But she could not stop looking at this woman's face, for it was a face she knew. After all these years Miriam knew that face.

Before the woman could look at her, Miriam impulsively whispered to the man who had brought her, "May we leave now? It is so crowded in here, so warm."

He protested, "We have only just arrived. I have not had sufficient wine. I wish to stay."

Miriam murmured against his ear, "My love, let us leave. I will offer you wine, and more besides."

He laughed and leaned to caress her, in the sight of all the guests. Miriam wanted to evade his touch, but she did not. He paid her well. "Soon," he said. "Soon. Only let us drink the health of my friend. Then we will go."

Suddenly there was a stir among the serving men. Miriam saw the steward of the feast go to the host and whisper something. The host looked annoyed and angry.

"I hope they have not run out of wine," one of Reuven's friends said.

Miriam, unable to hear the conversation that followed, watched a pantomime. The woman whom she recognized turned to speak to the man beside her. He turned away from her, almost rudely. But the woman spoke again, laying her hand on his own. Miriam watched the man nod. She thought he appeared reluctant. She saw him speak to the steward and she watched the steward speak to the serving men. Carrying their wine jars they went toward the large water vessels which stood just outside

11

the door. When they returned, one of them offered the steward a cup. He drank. Miriam saw a look of surprised pleasure cross his face. He nodded and once again they began to serve the wine.

When Miriam tasted the new wine she was astonished. She turned to her lover. "Have you ever tasted wine like this? It actually tastes the way ripe grapes smell. It's a miracle of delight."

He tasted his wine and blinked. "I have never before tasted such a vintage." He drained his cup. "Come. Let us ask where they got it." He pulled Miriam along with him to the place where his friend, the bridegroom, sat with his family.

He clapped his friend on the shoulder and said, "So, you saved the best of the wine until the last of the feast. What a splendid idea! We drink to your long life and joy and many sons. Later, when you have recovered your strength, you can tell us where you found wine like this."

Miriam felt the laughter, the sly, knowing glances of the guests. Usually she did not mind because she felt only scorn for others. But now she was embarrassed. In spite of herself she looked again at that familiar face. The woman returned the look. A surprised, loving smile touched her lips and eyes, and a silent message.

Then Miriam knew who the man must be, the man who looked at her sternly and with grief. She knew them both, the mother and her son. She felt their eyes on her as she left the wedding feast with her lover.

All that night, as she lay with the man who paid her to be his companion, she tried to exile from her mind the sight of the two who had once again stepped into her life, but she could not. Almost, she wished she had not tried to lure the man with a smile.

If I had known, she thought, *I would not have tried.* But, honest with herself, she was not sure. After all, he was a man. And she was the kind of woman she was.

She stared into the dark. Beside her Reuven murmured and stirred. She hoped he would not waken and want her again. She closed her eyes, but behind them she saw the face of the woman who had known her in that other life.

Tense and sleepless, Miriam told herself, *I will not think of it.* She touched the puckered scars which disfigured her left hand. *I will not remember it.* But a forgotten feeling rose in her, a longing so acute that she burned with it. She wanted to escape, to lose herself in sleep. But she was afraid to dream. She might, in a dream, see that child. The child she once had been.

2

"Don't hurt Miriam," Rachel coaxed her baby son as he tugged at the girl's hair.

Miriam smiled. "He doesn't hurt me." The baby boy grinned his toothless grin as Miriam scooped him up and blew on his soft stomach. He laughed aloud and when she stopped he clutched her hair and kicked.

"He wants you to do it again. Only a few months old, and already he knows what he wants," Rachel said fondly.

"Oh Benjamin, I do love you," Miriam told the laughing baby. "I wish I could stay here with you."

Rachel sounded uneasy as she said to Miriam, "It's getting late. Will your parents be needing you?"

Miriam drew back from the baby. "I didn't mean to stay so long." She tried to hide her fear by speaking naturally. "Good-bye, Benjamin. Maybe I'll see you again tomorrow."

She ran the short distance to the inn which was her home. When she rushed in her father greeted her with a blow which knocked her to the floor. She crouched at her father's feet, her tangled red-gold hair shielding her face. Her cheek burned from the force of her father's blow.

"Ten years old and still no good to anyone. If you can't be here when I need you, you'll wish you had never been born."

Sometimes Miriam already wished that. She could never do anything to please her parents.

Her mother pulled the girl to her feet. "Take the wine to those men in the corner." The harsh voice carried clearly even though the inn was full of noisy men, some already drunk, some only beginning their evening meal.

Miriam walked carefully, balancing the load which was too heavy for her. She dreaded those men in the corner, knowing that they would pinch her, touch her in ways she feared, if she were not quick enough to evade them.

She took them their wine and hurried back toward her mother, although she knew there was no real safety there. The inn was full, a rare event, since it usually did not do well. But this was a special occasion.

"Why does that half-Jewish tyrant, that Rome-lover make us travel so far to be enrolled?" she heard one traveler ask another.

Scornful laughter. "You didn't think he'd come to us, did you?"

"I'll have nothing left after I pay my taxes," another man complained.

"Then pay me now." The innkeeper was only half jesting.

The noise in the room was deafening. Smoke from the oil lamps mingled with cooking smells. Miriam's mother carried food; her father continually patted the leather pouch which was growing fat with coins. He called to Miriam, "Where are your brothers when I need them?"

Miriam had six brothers, three younger, three older

than herself. They were rough boys. The older ones were apprenticed to shepherds, and lucky to be apprenticed. The younger ones kept to themselves, like a skulk of fox puppies. It was her oldest brother whom Miriam feared. She had reason to fear him, but she kept that reason secret.

Now her mouth was dry as she tried to answer her father. The words came in a whisper. "They're in the fields with Laban and Ezra."

He moved toward her. "Speak up when you answer me. I've told you." He raised his hand and she cowered against the coming blow.

And then Miriam saw two people standing at the doorway of the inn. She knew that her father saw the couple, too. Miriam glanced at them. The woman looked very young. She did not speak, but her eyes met Miriam's with a silent message. Miriam shivered.

She saw that the woman was near her time to deliver. It was clear to Miriam that her back hurt. She had seen her own mother stand like that, to ease an aching back, in the weeks before her brothers were born.

"Have you room for us?" the man asked the innkeeper.

"We're full. You can see that. Every place is full." Again Miriam's father touched his money pouch. She thought he touched it almost as if he loved it. He had never touched her that way.

"But my wife . . . " the man at the door began.

The innkeeper was impatient. "I told you. We're full."

Miriam hardly ever spoke, especially not to her father. But now something made her speak. Was it the look in the woman's eyes? "They could stay in the barn," she said timidly, not looking at her father.

He seized her chin, forcing her face up, glowering at her. And then, even as he stood looking down at her, his expression changed. She saw slyness in his eyes, and greed. "Of course they can stay in the barn." His tone was oily, false, as if he cherished his daughter. "And you can make them comfortable."

He released her and turned to the man, asking him much more than a lodging in the barn was worth. The man did not argue, but paid at once. "Take them out there," her father said abruptly, showing no further interest in the couple.

Miriam liked the barn. It was a natural cave near the inn. Her father had made a crude door of branches to keep the wind out and the animals in. She spent much of her time there. Since her sixth year Miriam had been responsible for the care of the animals: a cow, a few chickens, a goat, and her favorite, the donkey. He was a patient little beast, and Miriam often talked to him. It seemed to her that he understood what she said, knew how she felt.

Now she took a small oil lamp and led the young woman and the man into the barn. "Don't be afraid of the animals," she told them. "They are all gentle."

"We won't," the man said.

Miriam piled hay and straw in heaps for them to lie on. "If you get cold," she told the woman, "you can cover yourself with hay. I sometimes do when I sleep out here. It scratches, but it's warm." It was the longest speech she had ever made.

The woman did not speak but she smiled at Miriam. Again Miriam shivered. She felt that smile as if it were a touch, the kind of touch she had never felt from her mother's hand. It made her want to cry, somehow.

18

As she left them, the man was trying to make the woman comfortable. He covered her with his own cloak. Miriam thought it strange that a man could be so tender.

Inside she went to the cooking corner and ladled stew into her bowl. She took some bread and started out with the food.

"Where are you going with that?" Her mother's voice was sharp. It always was.

"I haven't eaten yet," she told her mother. "It's too crowded in here. I'm going upstairs."

Her mother shrugged. The family rooms were over the inn. Miriam's was only a small loft in a corner. But she did not go up there. She took the food to the barn. "It's all I could get," she told them. "I hope it's enough."

"Thank you," the man said. The woman did not speak. Miriam knew her time was near, just from the way her face would change. Hurt marks crossed it and then smoothed out. Miriam had seen her mother's face like that. The man tried to help, something Miriam's father had never done. He pressed his hands against the woman's back, when the pains came, trying to ease her. Miriam studied his face. It puzzled her. She found herself liking this man, she who had never liked a boy or man before. Except her younger brothers when they were babies. Except Benjamin.

She left the food beside them, wishing she could stay, knowing she could not. Later, lying on her straw sleeping mat up in her loft, she was restless. Two things Miriam liked about her small loft. She had it to herself, and she could see the sky.

That night the sky was bright with stars. One star, more than the others, blazed, the way a single star some

19

times will. It seemed to Miriam that it was close enough to touch. And, drifting toward sleep, she thought she heard music. Not the kind she was used to, the whine of pipes and twang of strings, but quite a different kind of music. She thought it was the kind of sound stars might make if they could sing. Bright and blinding and far away.

At last, led by the stars' music, Miriam got up and went to the barn. The inn was full of shadows that threatened her. She thought of men lying in wait for her, and the things that could happen to her if she were caught by one of them. Still, she went, silently, secretly, as if something pulled her.

The baby had been born. The young mother had already wrapped it in cloths she must have brought with her. She lay on the floor, on the straw, the baby in her arms. She looked tired and weak. The man stood looking down at both of them.

Miriam heaped some clean hay in the cow's feeding box. "The baby could sleep here," she told the mother, "when you want to lay it down. I could put it here for you."

The mother smiled at Miriam. "I'll keep him with me now," she said. Then she asked, "Would you like to hold him for a moment?"

Miriam knew how to handle babies newly born. She had held her three younger brothers often enough. She took the baby from his mother. He was like any other newborn, his face looking old, his mouth puckering and mewing, his fingers curling and reaching.

Miriam put one of her fingers into his tiny hand and

felt the baby's fingers curl around her own. She smiled as she gave him back to his mother.

Then, hearing a commotion outside and recognizing the voices of her brothers, she hid in a shadowy corner of the barn. She did not want them to see her there.

Laban and Ezra, the two old shepherds, came in followed by three of Miriam's brothers. The oldest one was there, the one she feared and avoided. At first they all stared at the mother and the baby. Then Ezra and Laban stepped closer.

To Miriam's surprise, the two old men suddenly knelt on the rough floor. Ezra took off his filthy cap. Laban took his off, too, clutching it between his gnarled fingers. They knelt there, staring, waiting. Miriam's brothers shoved at each other and jostled. But soon they, too, were quiet.

After a while Laban turned and asked the man, "Is he a Savior, the baby? A Lord?"

Miriam's brothers snorted and guffawed, poking at each other.

"Why do you ask this?" The man sounded puzzled.

"Because the voices from the sky told us we would find a Savior here in this barn. A Lord. I've never seen a Lord." Laban grew excited. "And the star. Come out and look. It shines above the barn. They said to follow it, the voices did."

From her secret place in the shadows Miriam heard her oldest brother sneer, "The old man's daft. I heard no voices."

The man spoke kindly to Laban. "This is our son. My name is Joseph. My wife's name is Mary. Our home is in Nazareth, in Galilee. We have come here for the census."

Laban blinked and twisted his cap. "But the voices said

21

a Lord. They sang, too, but I could not understand the words."

Miriam heard her brothers muttering. She did not hear what they said, but she could guess. She knew that they would never hear voices from the sky. They would not listen. But she remembered the star music she had heard earlier, in her loft.

Ezra nodded and said, "It's true. The voices sang. They told us not to be afraid. We were afraid because the sky was so bright, but the voices told us not to be afraid. They told us to come here. So we came."

Again Miriam heard her brothers snickering.

Mary said, "Thank you for coming here to see our son. Now it is time for us to sleep." Miriam thought that she did not seem surprised or puzzled by anything Ezra and Laban had said.

The old men shuffled out, looking back at the baby as they went. Miriam's brothers left, too, pushing and shoving each other. Soon Miriam was alone again with the three in the barn.

Mary said, "You can come out now."

Miriam left the shadows and looked at the baby again. He had slept through the visit of the shepherds, but he was beginning to stir and mew. Miriam knew it was time for her to go so his mother could nurse him before they slept.

"Good night," she told them. "I'll bring you some breakfast in the morning."

"Thank you," the man said. "You are kind to us."

Then Mary asked, "What is your name?"

"My name is Miriam."

"Good night, then, Miriam," the girl-mother said.

Miriam went back to her loft, the feeling of the baby's fingers on her own, the smile of the mother still warming her. And the sound of a voice speaking her name as it had never been spoken before.

3

Drawn by the love which she felt all around her in the barn, Miriam spent as much time as she could there with Mary, Joseph, and the baby. She did her chores, dodged her parents and her brothers, and feasted on love.

"I'm sorry you have to stay out here," she said to Mary one night when she had stolen from her loft to be with them. "I know my father charges you too much."

"We're happy to have a place to stay," Joseph told her. "And you are so good to us that we could be living in a palace." A smile touched his kind face.

Miriam was embarrassed. She absently chewed on a strand of her curly hair. This barn a palace? To change the subject, she asked Mary, "Did you walk all the way from Nazareth?"

"No," the young mother said. "Good neighbors let me ride their donkey when I grew tired."

"I like our donkey," Miriam told her. "I pretend that he's my friend. I talk to him."

Joseph asked her, "Are none of your brothers friendly toward you?"

"No." Miriam's answer was immediate. "And my oldest brother . . . "

Joseph waited before he asked, "What about him?"

"I don't know. I'm afraid of him." To her horror Miriam found her throat tightening and her eyes filling with tears. She never cried, not even when her parents beat her. And she did not want to cry in front of these people. But she could not stop herself.

Mary placed her son in the manger and took Miriam into her arms. When the girl was calmer Mary said, "We four can be friends. And do you know that we share a name, you and I? Miriam and Mary are really the same. Our name means 'Bitterness' for it is like our word for that which is bitter. 'Marah.' Do you know the story of our ancestor, Moses, and his sister?"

Ashamed of her tears and her ignorance, Miriam did not answer. She only shook her head.

Mary, holding Miriam's hand in her own, told her, "Moses was born into the bitterness of captivity, in Egypt. His parents named his older sister Miriam, for she, too, had been born into captivity. Some day you will learn the whole story."

Miriam was filled with such a rush of joy that she thought she could not contain it. She shared a name with this new friend of hers. And Joseph was her friend, too. And the baby. Maybe they would all stay in Bethlehem and Miriam could leave the inn and live with them and be part of their family. Mary would tell her stories and
. . .

"Miriam." Joseph spoke her name. "Miriam, if you are truly afraid of your own brother, you must come to us if you need our help." He looked at Mary. "If we are still here."

"Oh please stay," she said. "Don't ever go away. You

could stay here in Bethlehem and I could live with you. I could help with the baby and . . . "

Joseph interrupted. "We will remain in Bethlehem for a while, at least." He looked at Mary and the baby. "For a while. And we will see each other often, although it would not be right for you to live with us, since your place is with your parents."

I wish you were my parents, Miriam thought.

Mary spoke softly. "But Joseph, your work in Nazareth. It will not wait."

"It will wait." The big man smiled. "I feel that we must not travel yet. Not until you are stronger. Not until our son is stronger."

It was almost as if the two of them had forgotten that Miriam was present, they talked so freely to each other. Yet Miriam felt that their words were veiled in a way she did not understand.

Mary said to Joseph, "You really mean that when I am stronger and our son is a bit older, we can return to Nazareth and the village gossip will have subsided. I can move about with my husband and our child and we and our families will hold their heads up again."

Joseph stroked his beard, silent for a long space before he answered. "No one could ever doubt your goodness, your purity."

"Not even you?"

"I least of all." Joseph's strong voice was gentle.

Miriam heard herself say, "Oh Mary, no one could be as good as you are. As kind."

The two of them looked at her in surprise, as if they had forgotten her while they were talking. Then Mary said,

"Thank you, Miriam. And now you must go back to your duties so that your parents will not be cross with you."

Reluctantly Miriam left them, looking back over her shoulder at the sleeping baby so warm and snug in his manger bed. It seemed to her that a glow of soft golden light surrounded him. The cave was dark, the flame of the oil lamps fitful. The golden light shone from the baby himself, and Miriam did not find it strange. Nothing could surprise her about a baby for whom stars sang.

One day Miriam heard her father tell her mother, "I'm going to let them stay in the barn for a while. The fellow says he's a carpenter and he offered to work for me in exchange for a place to stay." He laughed, that grating sound which had no merriment in it, the sound which always made Miriam uneasy. "But he'll pay me with coins, too. I made sure of that. I don't trust him."

Miriam's mother said, "It's not much of a place for a girl with a newborn. But I suppose it's better than nothing." She shrugged.

Miriam could scarcely contain her joy, but she did not speak. They would be so near that she could see them every day. She would be with them. They would . . .

She was jolted from her reverie by her father's harsh voice. "As for you, you still tend the animals and muck out the barn. And you don't spend all your time mooning over the baby."

She did not respond.

He rushed over and shook her so hard that her teeth hurt. "Do you understand? Answer me when I speak to you."

"Yes." But she knew that, even with the threat of her

father's anger hanging over her, she would spend all the time she could with the three of them. No matter what.

In the next months Miriam was happier than she had ever been. Joseph worked at repairing the inn, and when news of his skill spread, he was kept busy helping others in Bethlehem. Somehow he obtained enough wood to make a chair for Mary, and a table. The cave began to look like a rough home. The animals did not seem to mind their human companions. And Miriam herself felt at last that she was truly part of a family.

As Mary grew stronger, Miriam showed her the way to the well and helped her carry water back to the cave. Rachel often talked with them, and Benjamin began to walk. Miriam laughed at his wobbly, unsteady steps.

"See the baby, Benjamin," she would say. "You were once just as small as he is." And Benjamin would laugh and reach to pull Miriam's hair.

"And before too long the baby will be as big as you are," Rachel would say, caressing her son.

Miriam thought, *Oh, not too soon. I don't want them to go away.*

"Come, my Lamb," Mary would say to her hungry baby. "Let us go home and feed you." And they would go back to the cave. Miriam never heard Mary or Joseph call the baby by his name, not in all those first months of his life. *My Lamb,* they would say, or simply, *Son.*

Mary was still frail, and Miriam thought it strange. Her own mother was always up and at work a few days after her babies were born. But Mary seemed fragile. Miriam would often see Joseph glance at her with concern. But Mary never complained, and she tended her baby and their cave home carefully.

When the baby was little more than a year old he was walking precariously around the cave, laughing at the animals, petting their sides, their legs.

"Be careful," Miriam would tell him. "They are gentle, but they are much bigger than you."

But the cow only looked down with her liquid brown eyes, and the donkey patiently twitched its ears. The child never showed the slightest fear.

After he passed his first birthday he was lively and inquisitive, toddling around the inn-yard. Mary kept him as close to the barn as she could. He was saying a few words now. "Abba," he called Joseph. *Daddy.* And Mary was "Immie," *Mommie.* He could not manage to say Miriam, but he laughed up at her, and his laugh, his smile would melt Miriam so that she felt sometimes as if she were swimming in a sea of love.

One night she had crept down from her loft, because she could not help herself. She had gone to the barn just to see if they were still there, and safe.

"You are restless tonight, Miriam?" Mary asked.

"Yes. I don't know why. I had to know for sure that you were all right."

Mary nodded, her face serious, but she did not speak. Joseph said, "We are safe."

Miriam was relieved. The child slept soundly in the manger bed which was almost too small for him by now. They were all companionably silent together until suddenly Miriam said, "Listen. Do you hear something?"

The sound came again. The neighing of a horse, the clang of camel bells. "Somebody's coming."

As she had on the night when the baby was born, Miriam hid in the shadows where she could not be seen.

She knew she should be up in her loft, asleep, but she stayed. As she watched, three old men came into the barn, dressed for traveling. They walked stiffly, as if their bones hurt them.

Their clothing was rich. Two of them wore long cloaks trimmed with fur. One man was bearded and he wore a turban which was agleam with precious stones of every color. His rings gleamed, too. The third man was black. His cloak was trimmed with brightly colored feathers. Even in the dimness of the barn, Miriam felt their color.

She began to tremble. She knew these men were very important. What could they be doing in the barn? She could hardly breathe, her heart beat so fast in her chest. Even the animals were silent. The cow, chewing her cud, looked at the men with her mild brown eyes.

The three visitors stood for a while in silence, gazing at the child asleep in the cow's feeding box, and at his parents. The bearded man spoke. "We are students of the stars. Each of us set out on a journey, led by a star. We met, not by chance but by design, and we have traveled together long miles, to this place."

"You are priests?" Joseph asked.

"Some call us that. Others call us magi. We serve the mysteries of the heavens."

Then, just as Laban and Ezra had done earlier, they knelt beside the infant. Miriam heard their knees creak and crack when they knelt. Soon one of the men called out in a language which Miriam did not understand. At once three serving men carrying gifts came into the barn. Miriam was sure they were gifts, just from the way the servants carried them so carefully.

The first visitor, the oldest one, placed a small golden

casket on the floor beside the manger. Miriam thought it seemed to be heavy.

He spoke. "I, Gaspar, bring gold to the new king, for he should be crowned with gold." He lay full-length on the floor for a long moment. Mary and Joseph watched without speaking.

Miriam was astonished. The child a king? The old shepherds had asked if he were a Savior. A Lord. Now he was being called a king. She did not understand. But she knew that if that box were full of gold, it could have bought her father's inn and everything in it. And more.

The second man laid before the infant a container so beautiful that Miriam knew it must hold something precious.

"I, Melchior, have brought frankincense to honor the new king." He bowed to Mary when he had risen from his knees beside her son.

Mary did not speak, but Miriam saw her nod.

Then the black magus held high the box which he took from his servant. He said something in a strange language and prostrated himself before the baby. When he spoke again, it was in the language which Miriam understood.

"Balthazar brings myrrh to honor his dying, when the time comes for his death. For it will come, as it comes to each of us."

Miriam shivered. She wondered why he spoke of dying when the child was so young.

Mary said, "We thank you for your gifts to our son and for your journey."

Solemnly the three bowed. Then the oldest man turned to Joseph. "We paid our respects to King Herod on our way. He was not pleased to hear of a new monarch. We shall return to our homes by another route, as we were directed in a dream. It was in our reading of the stars that we learned of the birth of this child. He does not appear to be a king, but the stars do not lie. Nevertheless, be warned. Herod is a jealous ruler."

When the three had left and Miriam could no longer hear any sound outside, she came out of the shadows again and stared at the gifts. The boxes were gilded, incised with pictures of strange birds and beasts and plants. She would have liked to touch them.

For a long time no one spoke. Then Miriam asked, "What did they mean about King Herod? My father and the people who come to the inn don't like him. They call him a tyrant. I don't know what that means."

Before they could answer her she looked at the sleeping child and asked, "What did they mean? Is he really a . . . " She could hardly speak the word. "Is he really a king?"

It was Mary who answered. "He is our son. And he is the king of our hearts." She touched her child's head.

Joseph, too, looked at the baby. He did not look at the gifts. He bent to touch Mary. "Yes," he said. "He is our son."

4

The joy she felt in being with the family in the barn shielded Miriam from the abuses she suffered at the hands of her own family. Still, she often ached from her father's blows and she was always tired with the exertion of carrying loads too heavy for her and from the constant need to dodge chance encounters with the men who came and went.

One night, exhausted and spent, Miriam slept deeply. But she dreamed. She saw herself and the one who spoke to her, and in the way of dreamers, she knew that she dreamed.

Someone said her name. "Miriam. Miriam."

In her dream she wakened and saw, or thought she saw, the one who spoke. It was a creature who looked like a man, but he was so much more beautiful than any person she had ever seen that she could hardly believe he was real. Yet, in her dream she knew he was.

He was surrounded by light. He was made of light, in the appearance of a man. He had great, widespread wings, larger than the wings of any bird. They were not made of feathers, but of light which moved and trembled and swept circling arcs of radiance about him.

Miriam was afraid. His face was at the same time stern and kind. His eyes, it seemed to Miriam, knew her through and through. She felt that he knew everything: her fear of her father, her deep longing that her mother should love her, her dread of her oldest brother. Everything. In the dream she shivered.

"Miriam," he said, and his voice was not really a voice at all, but music which she understood. "I bring you a message. Listen well."

In the dream she asked, "Who are you?" Awake, she never would ..ave asked. She would have run away from him in terror.

"I am the Messenger," he said. "You must hurry to the barn and waken Joseph. Tell him he is to take the child and his mother now and flee. They must go down into Egypt. As once their ancestors lived in Egypt, so now they must be exiled there and live in a new captivity until it is safe for them to return to their home. Tell Joseph to go now, in all haste. He will believe you. You are to help them, for you are the only one who can."

In her dream Miriam stared at him, not knowing what to do or say.

"Miriam," he said again, his voice-music loving, sad, commanding. "This will cost you much. More than a child should have to pay." Then he touched her, in the dream, and she felt his touch like fire or like ice, and she was wrapped in his wings for a long moment until she thought she would die from the heat of it, or the cold. But she did not want him to let her go. Then, with a fading softness, he was gone and she awoke.

She did not hesitate. She ran to the barn, careful not to make a sound. They all slept. The child lay in the manger. Mary slept on the floor, Joseph beside her, his cloak spread over both of them.

Miriam touched him. "Wake up," she whispered. "Please wake up."

He woke with a great start and looked about him as if to seek for someone.

Then Miriam knew. "You've been dreaming," she said.

His eyes widened in alarm. "Yes, I have had a dream. I have been told to leave this place and go . . . "

"Into Egypt," Miriam said.

The whispering wakened Mary and she raised herself up, looking toward the manger where her son lay. "What is it?" she asked. "Miriam, why are you here? What has happened?"

Joseph told her, "Miriam and I have both been warned in a dream. It is time for us to go. We are no longer safe here."

Miriam said, "You have to go to Egypt. It is a long way. I have heard of people who were lost in the desert on the way. They say there was nothing left of them but their bones." She trembled with fear.

"We shall not be lost, Miriam," Joseph assured her. "Somehow we will be led, even through the desert."

"The Messenger said I was to help you," Miriam told him. "You have so far to go. To Egypt. I have never been there. Can I go, too? I could help. I wouldn't eat much, or be in the way. Oh, take me with you. I promise I won't be any trouble. Please, take me with you."

Mary said gently, "It would not be right for you to leave your home. We would like to have you come with us, but it would not be right." She picked up her son. "How shall

I walk all that distance into Egypt?" she asked Joseph. "Where will I find the strength? I feel so weak."

Then Miriam knew what she must do. She untied the donkey and gave the lead to Joseph. "Let them ride on his back," she said. "He will help you cross the desert. Maybe you will meet a caravan to help protect you."

Mary handed the sleeping infant to Miriam while Joseph helped her up to sit on the rough, shaggy back. Joseph said, "We cannot pay you. Our son has gold, but it is not ours to give. I fear that you will pay for this."

Miriam touched her lips to the child's head and held him up to his mother. She walked out into the shadows of the road with them. Suddenly she asked, "What is his name? You have never told me."

Mary said, "His name is Jesus."

How strange, Miriam thought, *that Mary's son and my own oldest brother should have the same name.* Whenever she spoke her brother's name, or heard it spoken, it sent a shudder of fear through her.

But the name of Mary's son, *Jesus.* It was as if she had never heard the name before, Mary said it so lovingly. Miriam reached to touch the sleeping infant one last time.

Joseph said, "We must go now. We thank you for all your kindness to us."

Miriam could not answer for the lump which filled her throat. Mary said, "Good-bye, Miriam. I hope that we will all meet again. We will not forget you. Remember us."

How could I ever forget you? Miriam thought. She watched until she could no longer see them. Then she went back to her loft.

Lying on her mat, looking out at the night sky, she tried

to remember exactly what the Messenger had looked like, half hoping that he would return to her and tell her to go with them. But perhaps he was there, guiding those three who had begun their journey away from her.

Why did you have to come? she asked the Messenger. *Why did you take them away? Why couldn't I go with them?*

But there was no answer.

*   *   *

Miriam's mother shook her awake the next morning saying crossly, "Are you going to sleep all day? There's work to do. Get up."

It was so early that the sun had barely risen. Miriam's first thought was of the family in the barn. With a lift of joy she told herself, *I'll take them their breakfast.*

Then she remembered, and her sorrow was a great lurching in her stomach. Even though she knew that her mother would be cross if she did not go directly to help her, Miriam went to the barn.

The cow gazed at her placidly. Doves cooed in the recesses of the cave. Rays of early morning sun slanted above the empty manger. They were really gone. No magic spell had been cast during the night to help them stay or to bring them back. And the donkey was gone, too. Her father was sure to be angry. Slowly, reluctantly, Miriam went back to the inn.

She was helping her mother when her father came raging in. "Those miserable people have taken their brat and gone, and they have stolen my donkey. You were the one who said to take them in," he said to Miriam. "Now look what's happened. Well, you'll pay for it." He hit her across the face so hard that she fell to the floor and lay there stunned.

"Thieves," her father roared. "I should have known it. They were thieves."

Miriam, who so seldom spoke to her father, did not want to speak now. But with an effort she raised herself from the floor and looked at him. "They are not thieves," she said. "They did not steal. They paid for everything. The barn, the food. They did not steal the donkey. I gave it to them." When she had spoken, Miriam wished that she could swallow the words, but they were said.

Her father was speechless, but not for long. When he did speak, his voice was quiet, and that quiet tone frightened Miriam more than his roaring had. "You gave it to them? My donkey?"

To Miriam his face looked like the face of a lion just before it leaps. Like the face of an evil spirit which she had met in a nightmare and was afraid to meet again.

"And was it yours to give?" His mouth barely moved to form the words; his whisper was soft.

"No."

Saying nothing more, he pulled Miriam up from the floor. Her face burned where he had struck it. Her arm ached from the tightness of his grip. He spoke again in that soft, threatening tone. "This may help you remember, the next time you think to give away something that is not yours."

40

Miriam knew that something terrible was going to happen to her. In a recess of her mind she heard Joseph say to her, *I fear that you will have to pay for this.* Miriam glanced toward her mother but she found no help there. Unmoving, the woman stared at her husband.

Then, standing back from the fire so that it would not burn him, Miriam's father thrust her left hand into the flames and held it there. She screamed. It seemed to Miriam that he held her there forever. Finally she heard her mother say her father's name, and then she remembered nothing more.

When she awoke, lying on her pallet up in the loft, Miriam's hand was burning. It was wrapped in cloth. She knew that her mother had put ointment on it, the kind she used when any of the family or any of the beasts suffered a mishap. Miriam herself had helped prepare the aloes.

She thought she would die of unbearable pain but she could not cry. The pain devoured her, as if it were alive. Nothing remained of Miriam but pain. And it was not only in her hand. It filled some inner part of her which she could not describe. She wanted someone to hold her, to comfort her. She felt very small and alone.

If Mary were here, she thought, *she would be sorry. She would look at me in that way she has and she would put her arms around me. I know she would.*

But Mary was gone. The three of them were gone. They were on their way to Egypt, and that could be the far edge of the world, for all Miriam knew. There was no one to comfort her.

If only they had taken her with them, this would not have happened. She would be far away from her parents

41

who had never wanted her, never loved her. She would be with three who did love her.

But maybe they did not want her, either. They had gone away without her. No one wanted her. And if those three had not come at all, she would not be lying in pain so great she did not know how to bear it. Thoughts ran across Miriam's mind, confusing her. Finally the tears began to run down her face. She tried to hold them back, restlessly moving her head from side to side. The tears ran into her mouth and she tasted them, salty and sharp. At last, exhausted by misery and loneliness, Miriam slept.

***

Each time her mother changed the dressing on her burned hand, Miriam thought the pain would kill her. But she did not die.

"Hold still," her mother would scold. "You brought this on yourself. Now you can live with it." Soon she was given tasks again. She felt tired all the time. She was surprised that her mother did not scream at her when she sometimes went to a corner of the inn to rest because she could no longer stand.

Once when she was resting, a traveler and his young son came in. They had been in Egypt. The boy looked at Miriam, and seeing her bandages he asked, "What happened to your hand?"

Before she could answer, Miriam's father said, "The stupid girl fell into the fire and burned herself."

A feeling which Miriam did not recognize at first stirred in her. Her cheeks grew hot. She wanted to scream at her father, but she did not speak.

The boy came to stand near her. He appeared to be about the age of one of her younger brothers. Although Miriam disliked and feared most boys because of her brothers, this one seemed friendly and curious, like a puppy, and she did not mind when he spoke to her.

"Does it hurt?" he asked.

"Of course it hurts."

"May I see it?"

Miriam wanted to show it to him, but she did not. "You wouldn't want to see it. The first time my mother saw it, after she unwrapped it to put on more salve, it made her sick."

The boy asked, "Did it make you sick, too?"

"No." She did not tell him that she had fainted. Instead she asked him, "Were you really in Egypt? You and your father?"

"Yes. Have you been there?"

"No." Miriam had never been out of Bethlehem, but she did not tell him that. "What is it like?"

The boy's dark eyes were wide with wonder, as if he saw again the marvels of which he spoke. "They think their kings are gods. They build monuments to honor them, monuments so high that they touch the sun."

"They can't touch the sun," Miriam interrupted. "Nothing is that high."

"Well, they almost do," the boy insisted. "And there is a huge beast made of stone. A lion with the head of a king,

43

and he guards the monuments and a city they have built for the dead kings."

"A city? For dead people?" Miriam was puzzled.

"Yes. And there are temples with columns so tall you can't see the tops, and they are painted with birds and beasts and flowers. I've never seen such things."

The boy grew more excited as he talked. "The Egyptians have many gods. Goddesses, too. They have the heads of animals or birds. And there is a river. You can't imagine such a river. But I didn't like the trip across the desert, coming here. The winds blew sand until we couldn't see. There were bones, too, just lying there. Bones of animals and of people."

"People?" Miriam shivered.

"Yes. The bones were all white. You couldn't tell who they had been. I didn't like it. It scared me."

Miriam remembered that Joseph had told her they would be safe, even crossing the desert. She wondered if she would ever see the three of them again. But a new thought entered her mind. If it had not been for them, she would not have been burned. And they didn't even know. It seemed to her that nothing was fair.

***

One day, not long after, her mother sent her to the well. Miriam wondered how she could manage to draw water using only one hand.

Suddenly she heard screams and the thundering of horses' hooves. She looked up to see their neighbor, Rachel, holding Benjamin and running in front of a mounted soldier. He looked enormously high, seated on his horse which reared and snorted. The soldier's helmet and armor gleamed bronze; his tunic was a blur of scarlet.

"Miriam," Rachel screamed, "help me. Help me."

The Roman soldier pulled up beside them. He leaped off his horse, tore the child out of Rachel's arms, and plunged his sword into the softness of the infant flesh. In horror, Miriam watched Benjamin's blood streaming. It soaked Rachel; it splattered Miriam where she stood.

Then Miriam saw Rachel's eyes roll back in her head and she fell to the ground, lying on top of her dead son. Miriam felt caught in a nightmare as she stood, unable to move. The road was full of running, screaming women, of blood streaming, and all the babies dead.

Miriam ran to the inn. Out of breath she cried, "They're killing the babies. The soldiers are killing the babies. They're all dead."

Miriam's mother said nothing. The sobbing girl pulled at her mother's sleeve. "Rachel's baby is dead. They're all dead."

The travelers stared at Miriam. And still her mother did not speak. Her face was expressionless.

Her father came in then, and he told what had happened. "I heard a Roman centurion explain their mission, as if he needed to explain anything. King Herod heard about an infant, a king, supposed to be born here in Bethlehem, and it made him nervous." He laughed, and the laughter grated along Miriam's spine.

"Anything makes Herod nervous if it threatens him. So

45

he thought to kill the infant king." He laughed again, in derision. "He ordered all our male babies to be slain, all those two years and under, in order to do away with the right one."

Then Miriam knew. Herod had been trying to kill the son of Mary and Joseph. The three magi had honored him as if he were a king, and they had warned Joseph about Herod. And the Messenger. He had known what was going to happen. That was the reason they had to escape into Egypt.

"Lucky for Herod and those soldiers that they killed no son of mine," she heard her father say. "I'd have shown them blood for blood."

The travelers murmured to each other.

Her father said, "Well, they were just soldiers, after all, following their orders."

One of the travelers muttered, "Yes, but they could ride away afterward."

That night, lying on the mat in her loft, Miriam dreamed and woke and dreamed again. Waking, she thought of the babies. Some of them, like Rachel's son, Miriam had held and tended for their mothers when she could be spared from her work at the inn. She had felt the softness of them, heard them laugh or cry. She had watched them begin to walk, tottering in their funny ways, falling and trying again. Now she would never see them. Never. Benjamin would never laugh and tug at her hair with his chubby fingers.

Miriam knew that Rachel and her husband had waited long years for their baby. He was their treasure. Just as Jesus was the treasure of Mary and Joseph. And now Rachel's baby was dead.

Dreaming, she saw the soldiers with their bright, sharp swords, their faces like stone. She saw the mothers, heard their screams as the babies were snatched from them and killed. And in her dream she saw Mary holding her baby son and weeping. Weeping as if he, too, were dead.

5

After the slaughter of the babies, a cloud hung over Bethlehem. The women, gathering at the well, looked at each other with eyes full of pain. Rachel stayed in her house. Miriam took water to her, but Rachel seldom spoke. It was as though her life had stopped.

At night when Miriam lay in her loft, it seemed to her that she could hear the muffled wailing of women. Her sleep was still filled with nightmares. She wondered whether it was all her fault. If she had not helped Mary and Joseph and Jesus, perhaps they would not have stayed in Bethlehem. Then Herod would not have killed the babies. Benjamin would still be alive. She could not tell anyone about the Messenger. No one would believe her. She had no one to talk to, and she bore a burden which no one shared.

Tending the animals in the barn, missing the little donkey, feeding the chickens, helping her mother as well as she could with one hand, Miriam's thoughts were always divided. Sometimes she would not hear her mother's orders. Then there would be slaps and screams. Often Miriam wondered what it would be like to be happy, to be loved as Rachel and her husband had loved Benjamin.

One night a traveler, Miriam's father, and her oldest brother were drinking wine together. Miriam was kept busy fetching and carrying. She tried to avoid the eyes which followed her. She stayed near her mother when she could, although her mother never seemed to notice her except to scold her.

As it had since that terrible day, the talk turned to the slaughter of the infants. The traveler asked, "How did it happen that the baby Herod wanted to kill was here? Why did it happen in Bethlehem?"

"It was the census," Miriam's father explained, his speech slurred, his eyes red and shifting. "They had come here to be counted. Their brat was born in my barn." He looked at Miriam who stood near her mother. "And why was it born in my barn?" His voice frightened Miriam. Her father stared at her silently. Then he said to her, "Come here."

Paralyzed with dread, she could not move.

"Come here, I said."

Her mother gave her a shove and the child went toward her father.

He did not touch her. He sat without moving, without speaking, just looking at her. The traveler stared at her and so did her oldest brother. Miriam felt as if she were surrounded by wild beasts. Her heart began to thump in her chest.

At last her father spoke, his voice thick with wine and anger. "Look at her," he said. "Look at her." He spat at Miriam each time he spoke. "She is the one who told me to let them stay in the barn. She is the one."

50

Miriam thought that she would suffocate with fear. She looked down. Her hands trembled. Her legs felt as weak as if they had no bones in them.

"She is the one," her father said. "This worthless girl." Miriam felt the loathing in his tone.

"Look at her," her father spat again. "She is the one who gave them the donkey so that they could get away. She gave them *my* donkey."

Miriam could feel his rage increasing with each word. And she could feel her heart pounding. *Will he kill me now?* she wondered. *Why doesn't my mother help me?*

The drunken traveler laughed, a short, cruel sound. "She's got a mind of her own, that one has. And some day she's going to be a beauty."

Then Miriam's father stood, swaying drunkenly above her. He seized her hair and lifted her from the ground. She thought her scalp would tear.

"Take her if you want her," he said to the traveler sitting at the table. "She's worthless except to be used by anyone who wants to use her. Take her." He let Miriam fall then, and kicked her toward the man. Miriam's mother started to move toward her, but her husband motioned her away.

Miriam shut her eyes against the horror. She was only a child, her body smooth as an eggshell, unripe and tender. She was aware of the traveler above her, of tearing pain, the smell of her own blood and other odors which gagged her.

And then, her brother. When she tried to resist him he hit her, and when she could not stop screaming, he hit her again and again until, after a while, she sank into the dark.

***

Miriam opened her eyes. Her mother stood beside her with a cup of broth. Miriam's body ached. Even the pain in her hand was not as sharp as this pain which filled her secret places. She was afraid to breathe for fear that she would find a new spot which hurt.

"Drink some of this," her mother said, not unkindly.

Miriam was surprised at her tone. She looked at her mother. As she watched, that familiar face grew large and then receded to become pinpoint small. Her mother had let this happen to her. She didn't even try to stop it. Miriam closed her eyes against her mother's face.

She felt an arm behind her shoulders, raising her up. She cried out with the pain.

"Here. Sip a bit of this," her mother said again.

Miriam closed her lips tightly and turned her head.

"Have it your own way." The voice was rough again. "I'll leave it here."

When her mother had gone, Miriam sniffed the broth. It smelled good. She drank it all and slept again. When she wakened, she saw her brother grinning down at her. She began to tremble, partly with fear, partly with rage.

Suddenly Miriam's father came to the loft and roared at her brother, "I told you. Stay away from her."

Still grinning, Miriam's brother turned and left. Her father looked at her and she thought that the look held something of shame. But she closed her eyes so that she would not have to see him. When she opened her eyes again he was gone.

52

In the days that followed, Miriam lay on her mat looking out at the sky. She watched the day change. The sky grew bright with dawn, hot with noon, cooler with the setting of the sun, and mysterious with stars and the bright moon.

But nothing moved her. She could not make any pictures in her head, as she once had, of the wonders of Egypt. No pictures of the faces of the three she had come to love. For a long while she felt nothing at all except the pain in her body.

Once, when her brother looked in at her again, his voice was cruel. "What's all the fuss about?" he sneered. "You weren't even worth the taking." Miriam weakly threw a cup at him and he laughed, dodging it.

And one day when Miriam awoke, she was surprised to see Rachel standing in her loft, her eyes dark with grief, shadowed with sleeplessness.

"Miriam, I heard what happened." Her voice was soft and kind. "It is a shameful thing."

Miriam looked at her, this woman whose child had been murdered.

"It was not your fault," Rachel said, "This thing that happened to our babies."

Miriam noticed strands of white in Rachel's hair. They had not been there before.

"Miriam," Rachel said again, "do you hear me? It was not your fault. Not any of it. You must not blame yourself."

Still Miriam could not speak. She was numb to everything except her own pain. Something in her wanted to respond to Rachel, but she could not. She closed her eyes and later, when she opened them, she was alone again.

Gradually, in the days that followed, a new feeling began to pervade Miriam. A deadly chill moved along her body, out her arms, across her breast, and into her head. When finally everything was frozen, she was impervious to all feeling, even to pain.

Then something took root in the cold and began to grow. As her body slowly healed, it was filled with unremitting hate. She thought of the three who had caused all this, only because she had tried to help them. Anger and hate burned inside her, then, as fiercely as the fire which had burned her hand for their sake.

The fire annealed the inner ice and she turned to stone. She became a stone child with a core of hate seething and bubbling within.

I curse them all, Miriam said quietly, between her clenched teeth. *I curse my father and my mother. I curse my brother. I curse all men. I'll make them pay for what they've done to me. When I am a woman I will make them pay.*

And I will forget Mary and Joseph and Jesus. I will never think of them again.

So every day Miriam cursed her family and all men. Sometimes in her memory she caught a shadow of Mary's face, loving and kind. Or she saw Joseph helping Mary the night the baby was born. Or the tender, throbbing top of the baby's head and his smile.

But she thrust these memories aside and fed on hate. *I will never forgive any of them,* she vowed. *Never.*

6

"It's time you stopped feeling sorry for yourself," Miriam's mother told her one morning. "You've stayed up here long enough. There's work for you to do. I can't do it all by myself."

Miriam gave her mother a look so stony and unresponsive that it stopped the woman's words. She helped her daughter walk downstairs. When Miriam felt that she could stand alone she shrugged off her mother's hand.

"Go stir the soup," her mother said, her tone ugly, "if you think you're strong enough for that."

Miriam stared at her, not allowing anything to show through her stone mask but the fury in her eyes. She stared until her mother turned away.

Miriam's father, seeing her, acted uneasy. He looked first toward her and then away. Then, standing with his feet apart, he glared at her. She pretended he was nobody and looked past him.

Soon he snarled, "Get to work. Earn your keep."

She turned her stone mask his way and let her eyes glow with the force of her hate, and he left the room without speaking to her again.

For weeks any small amount of physical effort exhausted Miriam. She felt as if her very bones had turned soft. The sight of her brothers nauseated her, and especially the look on her oldest brother's face whenever she met him. Once, when no one was near the cooking place she looked for a knife, one as sharp as her mother's tongue, honed and lethal. When she found it she took it with her up to her loft, not with any real plan of using it, only for the comfort of its presence.

One night Miriam wakened to see her brother looking down at her. Her heart began to pound. Her mouth was dry with fear. In the light of his oil lamp she saw his leering, ugly face. He reached to touch her. She took the knife from its hiding place and, quick as a striking snake, she slashed him across the face. She saw his surprise, saw him touch his cheek and then look at the blood on his fingers.

She dared him with her eyes and hissed, "Come up here again, try to touch me, and I will kill you. I will kill you one night when you are asleep. I am not big or old, but I am clever and quiet. I swear to you, I will kill you."

He laughed, but it was not a mirthful sound. It was a coward's laugh, when he pretends courage. Or the laugh of a bully when he has someone smaller to torment.

From that night, he stayed away from Miriam. His wound healed in time, and he had a livid scar. Miriam rejoiced each time she saw it. It was not as bad as the scars on her hand, but at least she had put it there. It made a path from the corner of his left eye across to his nose.

She never spoke her brother's name.

People in the village shunned Miriam as if they held her responsible for the cloud which hung over Bethlehem, the deaths of the baby boys. She spoke to no one, and she was content that no one spoke to her.

Sometimes, in a dream, she would see the face of Mary, looking at her with love. Or she would see the baby smiling at her. Then she would waken and think, *They lied. Their smiles lied to me.* But part of her mourned that she was made of stone, that rage simmered within her. Sometimes she wondered what it would be like to be an ordinary child.

Only in the barn with the animals did she feel safe. Only then could she lay aside her mask and bank the flames of her hate. In stroking the beasts, in talking to them, gentling and feeding them, she felt relief. They repaid her with a kind of faithfulness.

By the time Miriam was twelve, she knew that she was more comely than other girls she saw at the well. By the time she was thirteen, everyone knew that she was beautiful.

She was tall for a girl, and lithe. Her amber eyes gleamed like cat's eyes. Sometimes they seemed to throw off sparks. Her red-gold hair lay thick and lustrous along her shoulders. Her skin was smooth and it glowed as if the invisible fire which burned within her touched it with gold.

She was flawed only in her hand. She managed to hide it most of the time. But she began to realize that it was not her hand at which people stared. Especially men.

Every day, when Miriam drew water at the well, she furtively watched the people who passed by. The only woman who spoke to her was Rachel. She had finally borne another son.

"Miriam," she would say, "will you hold the baby for me while I draw water?"

But Miriam would not. She had nothing against children and she was afraid that she might taint one of them by her very touch. She could not forget what had happened. She had loved Jesus and his parents had taken him away. She had loved Benjamin and he was dead.

When she was fifteen she realized the effect her beauty had upon the men who looked at her. She began to formulate her plan. *I will use men,* she thought, *as I was used. I will find ways to make them pay for what was done to me.*

She settled upon a man whom she had noticed because he often covertly noticed her. He was old, like her father, but he was dressed in rich clothing and he looked important. At first she acted humble when he passed, pulling her shawl modestly around her face, but not hiding it too much. She would step aside so that he could pass easily, but still close to her.

"Good morning," she said to him respectfully one day, when their eyes met. Her voice was soft and smooth and honeyed.

He looked at her, but he did not answer and quickly turned away. So the next day she did not speak. Then he spoke first. "Good morning, child."

Child! she thought. *I'm as old as anyone can be.* But she smiled and said, "Good morning."

One day he asked her name.

"My name is Miriam," she whispered.

"Miriam. It is a lovely name."

She smiled, secretly amused as he appeared to search for something else to say.

"Miriam," he caressed the name. "Do you know that Miriam was also the name of the sister of our ancestor, Moses?" His breath came faster and Miriam was sure that he was not thinking about anyone's ancestors.

She looked at him with wide, clear eyes, innocent and modest. Then she looked down again. "No, sir. Who was Moses?" For an instant she remembered Mary's words about the other Miriam. But she forced herself to forget at once.

The man seemed astonished. "Do you really not know?"

"Forgive me, sir, but I am ignorant." She sighed and looked into his eyes. "I wish I were not so ignorant. But there is no one to teach me."

"Who are your parents?"

"The innkeepers."

That was enough. One day soon after, Miriam's father said to her, "You are to work in the house of Nathan bar Judah. You will give me your wages. He says he wants to teach you, for you are bright enough to learn." He laughed. "These pious men with their long faces and their synagogues. You be careful what he teaches you."

She stared coldly at her father. He growled something she did not hear, and walked away from her.

So Miriam went to live in the house of Nathan and his barren wife, Esther. Esther spent most of her time moping, bewailing her childlessness, and visiting her friends. She was drab, and Miriam expended no energy in hating her. But it was no effort to hate Nathan. He was a man. Miriam listened patiently when he instructed her about Moses and Abraham, Isaac and Jacob. He told her about

59

King David, too, whose town was Bethlehem. And he told her about his God.

"His name is sacred," Nathan told her, "and it is not to be spoken. He is the One God, may his name be praised."

"Where does he live?" Miriam asked Nathan.

"Poor, ignorant child," Nathan answered. "The whole universe is his home, for he created it. And we must live by his laws."

"What laws?" Miriam asked.

Nathan shook his head in disbelief. "Do you not even know the Law?" he asked her.

"How could she know?" Esther said. "No one has taught her. Tell her."

"God gave the Law to Moses upon Mount Horeb," Nathan explained to Miriam. She pretended to be vitally interested in all he said, her eyes never leaving his own except to look at his lips.

"We must obey the laws." Nathan seemed to have trouble speaking. "Some of the Laws the Great One gave to Moses are, 'Thou shalt not steal. Thou shall do no murder. Thou shalt not covet. Thou shalt not commit adultery."

Still Miriam stared at him, apparently enraptured. Some of his words seemed to choke him, and she thought she knew why.

"Our God has given us the Law for our greatest good," Nathan told Miriam and his wife. "He gives us his gifts so that good desires may overcome evil desires. He places his gifts within our hearts so that we may live upright, blameless lives, dwelling within his Law. Our God is altogether merciful and gracious."

Miriam believed none of it, but she hid her disbelief.

Esther broke in, "If our God is truly gracious and merciful, why has he not given me a son? He was gracious to our ancestor, Sarah. He gave her a son in her old age. Why can he not give me a son, too? Is it that I am unworthy?" She wailed and hit her breast until Miriam winced.

Nathan's voice was stern. "You must not question the Almighty's will. He is all-powerful and he does what he will do."

Miriam thought they were foolish. Even she knew that, whoever their god might be, he did not give sons. She knew what men and women did to beget. And she was sure Nathan knew that she knew. She often managed to be so close to him that he had to brush against her to pass by.

Once he said, "Miriam, let me be a father to you. I know the cruelty of your own. The whole village knows something of your unhappy childhood. But all families are not like that. Most parents love their children. I have no child of my own. Let me be your father."

Miriam lowered her eyes and said, "You are good to me." But she did not want another father. So she continued her patient, subtle seduction of Nathan.

She waited until she thought the time was right, months after she had gone into the house of Nathan and Esther to be their servant. It was summer with bees humming and the scent of oleander heavy on the air. Esther had gone to another village to visit.

That morning Miriam performed all her duties, humming as she worked. She swept and scrubbed, she ground the corn, and she prepared the noon meal. She served

61

Nathan, kneeling before him, close enough that he could smell the fragrance of her shining hair, of her healthy young flesh. At the end of the meal she offered him ripe figs, and grapes with a moist, dusky bloom on them.

He took the basket from her and set it down. He took her hands into his own. Looking at the scarred hand he asked gently, "How did this happen, Miriam?" He did not shrink from the terrible scars, or show disgust.

She allowed tears to come into her eyes. "I was burned as a young child." Her voice was soft and filled with woe. "I regret that I am not a perfect servant to my master."

"My poor child. How terribly it must have hurt you, a burn which could leave scars like these." He touched his lips to the scars.

Miriam forced herself not to shudder as she felt the hair of his beard brush her skin. She fixed her tear-filled eyes on his and whispered, "My master is so kind. So kind." Then she gently drew her hands away from him, still looking at him. When she heard his breath quicken she laid aside her shawl, letting her hair fall free and loose. "I would like to please my master," she said.

She remained there, kneeling at his feet, her luminous eyes fixed on his, her lovely face near enough to touch.

He groaned. "Miriam." He reached to touch her cheek. He drew his hand away as if her skin burned him. He said her name again. "Miriam. You are so beautiful." Then, as if he could no longer fight himself, he picked her up and carried her to the sleeping place he shared with Esther. Miriam was glad that he was gentle. Compared to the pain she had felt before, from the traveler and her own brother, this pain was nothing, although she did not like the things he did to her.

62

When it was done, Nathan cried out, "Yahweh, forgive me. Miriam, forgive me." He began to pray, swaying back and forth, "Yahweh, forgive me. Forgive me."

Miriam dressed herself slowly and left him there kneeling and swaying. *He spoke the name of his god,* she thought. *It was I who made him speak it.* She went up to her own small room on the roof and tore her clothing. She gave herself a few scratches on her arms and face, carefully, so that her skin should not be scarred.

Then, half-naked, she ran through the street, wailing loudly. People saw her and followed her through the heat and the dust to the inn. She found her father and her oldest brother there, drinking wine. The townspeople clustered around.

"He hurt me," Miriam shrieked. "Nathan hurt me. He hurt me." She wailed and screamed.

Her father and brother stared at her. Then her father asked her, "He has taken you?"

"Yes. It was just like the time when you gave me to . . . " As if it pained her too much to finish speaking, Miriam only wailed. Between screams she stole looks at her father and her brother. She thought she could see her father think, *Money.* But her brother was drunk. His eyes were inflamed and crazy as he looked at her. She saw lust in those wild eyes. *He wants me,* she thought, *and he is furious that another man has had me.* Suddenly he lunged toward her.

Miriam screamed. "Don't hurt me. He is the one who did it. Don't hurt me again."

Her brother glowered at her. He looked more like a beast than a man. The scar she had given him distorted his face. He swayed above her, drunkenly. "He'll pay. I'll make the old fool pay."

Miriam knew that it was not from any love of her that her brother rushed to Nathan in mindless rage. It was only his love of violence and his desire for her that drove him to commit his first murder.

Miriam was fiercely triumphant at the thought that she had ruined Nathan, that she had cost him his honor and his life. And she had caused her brother to become a murderer. But somehow, despite the new sense of power which filled her, Miriam felt no real joy. Only bitterness. Only the constant stony cold.

**

Despite the disgrace Nathan had brought upon himself by his actions toward Miriam, he had been a respected man in Bethlehem. His wife, Esther, bereft and desperate, demanded justice.

One night, secretly, Miriam's brother left Bethlehem and no one knew where he had gone. Nor cared, for that matter. But the villagers avoided the inn. No one spoke to Miriam, but they had not spoken before, and she did not care.

When a caravan master came to the inn and Miriam's father saw him watching his daughter, he asked the man, "Do you want her?"

The caravan master studied her. Miriam felt his eyes measuring her. She looked at him scornfully.

"How much?" The man asked her father.

The innkeeper named a price.

"Too much." The caravan master seized Miriam's scarred hand. "She's flawed."

And so they haggled. At last Miriam's father consented to a price. "But you have to take her with you," he said. "And be sure she never comes back."

Her mother did nothing to stop her going. She did not even look at her daughter. Miriam knew that she was not really a person at all, but only a thing to be bought and sold.

So, at fifteen, Miriam became the property of a harsh man who used her badly. Aching, sometimes, with pain which she could hardly bear, she would not permit herself to cry. She only fed upon her inner reserves of fury, waiting until the time would come when she could find a way to use and not be used. She knew that time would come.

The caravan crossed the desert into Egypt. The trip was terrifying and endless. Caught in storms in which sand blew into her eyes, her ears, her mouth, blinding, deafening and choking her, Miriam thought of the three who had crossed this desert before her. She would see the bleached bones in the sand and wonder whose they were. Had the three traveled safely to their destination? She would catch an inner vision of their faces, would remember the feeling which had warmed and nourished her when she had been with them. But they had left her, and she had vowed to forget them.

It was in Egypt that Miriam found her chance. She was sitting alone one day under a palm tree, waiting for her master. She clasped her knees with her arms and rested her head upon them. Suddenly she felt a touch on her hair. She looked up to see an Egyptian staring down at her. He wore a white skirted garment draped at shoulder and waist. Around his neck was a massive necklace of flat blue and gold stones. His black hair was short and he was clean-shaven. Miriam stared at him.

At that moment her master came toward them. "What do you want?" he asked the Egyptian.

"Is she yours?"

"She is mine."

"Her hair," the Egyptian said. "I've never seen such hair. Red and gold. Our women have black hair. But this . . . " And then he asked, "Will you sell her?"

"For a price."

The two men haggled over her, and Miriam, feeling nothing, neither spoke nor moved. Finally she went with the Egyptian. The caravan master laughed as she left him. "You'll be disappointed," he scoffed. "But she does have spirit."

The wealthy Egyptian noble took Miriam to a dwelling of sun-baked brick, richly furnished and airy. He had a serving woman teach her how to bathe, how to anoint herself, how to rim her eyes with kohl and use the other cosmetics he purchased for her. He himself taught her how to please him.

Miriam quickly learned the art of pretense. She saw that it pleased him if she seemed to be moved by his passion, and she learned to feign her responses to him.

She was given the freedom of the estate, to wander where she liked. She found it soothing to sit in the formal garden, looking at the cool water of the pool which was surrounded by palm trees. Sometimes she went into the workrooms, the kitchen, with its scent of fresh bread, the brewery with its acrid, pungent odors, the stables. No one ever spoke to her. She never asked whether her master had a wife and she never asked the name of the city where her master sometimes took her.

He bought her beautiful clothing, jewels for her neck and ears, rings, bracelets and anklets. One night after she had pleased him especially he asked her, "What gift have I not given you that you would enjoy?"

Miriam did not even have to think about it. "A few coins of my own. A few coins so that I may buy trinkets and sweet ointments." *And to save,* she thought, *so that some day I may be free.*

He left her, to return with a handful of gold coins which he sifted through his fingers in a bright shower down upon her body.

She found the shops which sold perfumed ointments and attars. She never could get enough of their fragrance.

"But you bought ointment yesterday," her master said on a morning when she showed him still another vial. "Why do you need more?"

She shrugged. "I love perfumes. I can't get enough. Perhaps they will help me forget the smells of my childhood."

He brushed the hair back from her forehead. "What smells? Were they so bad?"

"Yes," she answered briefly. She touched the attar to her throat, her brow, her wrists, and she sniffed her own skin.

Her master laughed and embraced her. He liked showing her the wonders which the young boy in the inn had

67

spoken of so long ago. "See the pyramids. Each stone weighs more than you can possibly imagine. And the Sphinx. The guardian of the city of the dead. Look. His face is that of a king."

Sometimes Miriam would look up at the statues of kings and queens. She would study their faces and wonder about them. Had they been real people? Had they loved and hated? But they only looked past her into space, their eyes blank, their gaze severe and aristocratic.

"What do you think of them?" her master asked her.

"I wonder what they were like. What did they think about? Were they real?"

"They were real," her master told her. "The kings were considered to be gods. They spent their time mainly in preparing for the next life."

"The next life?" Miriam was puzzled.

"Yes, you ignorant child." Her master fondly scolded her. "The ancient ones believed that another life waits beyond this one. A life in which they would need all the treasures they possessed here. So they were buried with their clothing, their jewels and trinkets, even food for the journey. Their bodies were preserved so that their souls could return to them in order to rest."

"It's very strange," Miriam said. "Do you believe it is all true?"

He said, "Who knows? As for me, this life is enough, if you are with me to share it."

It is enough for me, too, Miriam thought. *One life is quite enough. And when it is over, I will be glad.* She had so often wished for death that she could not imagine anyone wanting still another life.

Miriam sometimes walked alone beside the river,

68

watching the boats, hearing the winding, nasal songs of the boatmen, looking at the outline of the pyramids against the intense blue of the sky.

One day, idly watching the people who walked along the shore, the donkeys with their burdens, she saw a small girl sitting on the ground crying bitterly.

First Miriam thought, *She is nothing to me.* Then something made her move toward the child. She was about ten years old. Her face was dirty, her nose running, her hair matted. Her clothes were rags. Her arms and legs were like brown twigs. She ignored the flies which swarmed around her, settling on her eyes and her lips.

Miriam stared at her. Then, taking a golden bracelet from her arm, she held it out to the child. "Here," she said crossly. "Wear it or sell it, but stop sniveling. That will get you nowhere."

The girl looked at Miriam as if she did not understand. Then a smile warmed her dirty face. She seized Miriam's left hand and covered it with kisses. Miriam snatched the scarred hand away. But the child took it again, looked at it, stroked it, and laid it against her cheek. Then, clutching the bracelet, she ran away.

The stone center within Miriam did not yield, nor did the constant flame of her rage abate, but, watching the small girl disappear, Miriam was reminded of another child, a child of ten, whom no one had loved. Not until three strangers had come into her life. But Miriam shook off the memory. She could not love this child. She could not love anyone. She had forgotten how.

And so the years melted into each other. Miriam went from man to wealthy man, becoming more and more successful in the arts she cultivated. Her beauty grew, and with it her fame. She became notorious, sought after because she was skilled in those arts most cherished by the men whom she used and scorned. She saved much of the gold which she now demanded and received.

Her only physical flaw was her hand, ugly and puckered with scars. She was adroit at hiding it, and she knew that it was not her hand which men noticed.

But Miriam herself could not ignore or forget it. She could never forget the way in which it had become flawed. She could never forget the fierceness of the fire which had burned it nor the man who had caused the burns, nor the ones for whose sake she had suffered.

The fire which burned in Miriam was her bright companion throughout her life. The men who desired her, whom she used, saw a woman of great beauty. A woman whose amber eyes held mystery, whose hair was a glory, whose appearance was striking. They did not suspect that inside the woman they adored burned a rage so hot it could have destroyed them.

The damaged child became a slave, the slave girl became a courtesan, sought after, showered with gift and treasure, legendary in her own time. And, in spite of the triumph she felt each time she captured the love of a man whom she despised, she was unmoved by anything. The stone child had become a stone woman, beautiful and desolate.

7

After the wedding at Cana, the small town in the hills of Galilee, Miriam would lie awake, on the transparent edge of sleep, hours on end. She would listen to the night sounds: the owl's call, the rodents which are the owls' prey shrieking their small, desperate farewells. Or she would hear the cries from her own heart.

Her heart had had no language of its own for so long that she did not know how to listen to it. She had chosen her life. She thought her heart was dead. And now, because of two people whose eyes would not let her go, she was forced to begin listening to her inner voices.

The look Jesus had turned upon her as they sat at the wedding, the look so stern and yet loving. She had seen it before in the radiant face of the Messenger. But the grief? Why should Jesus grieve on her account? He could not know what her life had been. What it was.

In such a town as Cana news traveled fast. Reuven told her of conversations he had had with friends concerning the wine at the wedding. "One would think there had been a miracle," he laughed. "That wine was so delectable. Our host is sly. He is not willing to share with us the

71

origin of that vintage nor the name of the vintner. He only smiles and says, 'We are glad it pleased you.' "

Miriam sighed. "I am weary of the whole thing. Take me away from this town, my love. Let us go somewhere new."

He was surprised. "But I live here. I can't leave my home and my family. Not even for you."

What does it matter? Miriam thought. *One man is like another.*

Only one man seemed to her to be unlike the others, and she would like to be far away from him. The very sight of him made her uneasy. As she had promised herself in that childhood life so long ago, now she tried to keep the promise to forget him.

So Miriam let it be known that she was free to make a new attachment. Her next lover took her to a place beside Lake Gennesaret. He was a young man, ardent and ecstatic, pouring out his declarations of undying love. Miriam was restless. It was increasingly difficult to respond to his fervent demands, even to remember his name. Aaron? Jacob?

On a day when she was alone, she wanted to be truly solitary so she walked away from the house and into the countryside. She did not even want to hear the sound of the water. She wanted to be quiet, to escape from everything. She was tired. Tired, most of all, of her own body.

She sat under a tree, leaning against it, feeling the solid earth with the palms of her hands. She smelled the freshness of green things and blossoms, she heard the bees.

She had begun to feel calm when all at once a man came leaping toward her. It was as if he danced. He leaped into the air, he turned in circles, flinging out his arms, throwing back his head, and crying out. When Miriam saw his face she knew that he cried for happiness. His face was that of one completely joyful.

At first he did not see Miriam. When he saw her he approached, still dancing, still weeping. She was not afraid. Although she had never felt such joy, she recognized it in him.

Suddenly he knelt before her. He pushed back the sleeves of his garment and held out his hands to her. "Look at me," he said. "Look at me. What do you see? Tell me. What do you see?"

She glanced at his hands and arms. Then, looking into his face she said, "I do not see anything."

He turned his hands over, palms up and then palms down. He rubbed the skin of his arms with his hands as if he touched a precious surface which delighted him.

"Look," he said again. "Look. See. I am clean."

"Yes," Miriam said, humoring him. "I see. You are clean."

In an abrupt change of mood the man put his face in his hands and wept, swaying back and forth. Still, Miriam felt that he was not unhappy. She asked him, "Why do you weep?"

"Because I am clean," he said, tears running down his face.

Miriam was puzzled. "Is it so strange, then, for you to be clean? And why are you weeping?"

Still kneeling, he lifted his hands toward the sky, lifted his face toward the light of that clear summer afternoon and said, "I am clean. He has healed me. I am clean, new, alive." Impulsively he sat on the ground in front of

Miriam, clasping his knees with his hands, rocking back and forth.

"Look at me," he said again. "Do I look like a leper?"

She laughed. "You know that you do not look like a leper. Are you a bit mad today?" She reached to touch his face. It was as if she touched a child, with no thought of seduction, although he was a man, not a child, and he was handsome and virile.

He became very still then, and with his own hand he touched his cheek where Miriam had touched it. It seemed to Miriam that he stopped breathing. Then he said, "You are the first woman to touch me in more years than I can remember. No one touches a leper." And again he wept.

Of course no one touches a leper, Miriam thought. *They are unclean by reason of their sins. I have sometimes thought that if sin made one a leper, I should be far advanced in leprosy.* "But I do not understand," she said. "One is a leper for all time, if one is a leper at all."

"No longer," he said. "No longer. There is one who cures. Today I have met him. Today I am cured."

Miriam shivered. She knew what he was going to say. And as they sat together on the ground with the sounds of summer all around them, he told what had happened to him.

"I had heard about this man. He has been traveling through Galilee with a few of his friends. He is quiet, for a rabbi, and not puffed up. He talks about strange new things. Wherever he goes people gather around him. He heals the sick. I had heard about that. He casts out demons and he cures diseases. There's nothing new about that. Other healers do the same.

74

"But this man is different. I followed him, too. I stayed on the fringes, of course. Often people threw stones at me to make me move. But something made me want to stay near him. I began to think, while I listened to him, while I saw his face, that he could heal even me."

Miriam broke in. "But that is not possible. No one has ever cured a leper." Something in her did not want it to be true, even though she saw the joy in this man's face. Perhaps he had only thought he was diseased.

"I know," he said. "But listen. Today while he was talking, I was bold. The people called out 'Leper, leper,' and threw stones. But I made my way to him. I knelt at his feet and I said to him, 'If you will, you can make me clean.' It was a bold thing to do, I know. But I believed with all my heart that he could heal me.

"He looked at me with such pity and love as I have not felt since I was born. I held out my hands to him, half-eaten away and disgusting, and I pleaded with my eyes.

"His look entered me like a sword or like the sun itself. He stretched out his hands toward me and I swear to you that heat came out of them. But it was not a destructive heat."

Miriam felt the old anguish. She pulled the sleeve of her garment down to cover her scarred hand.

The man said thoughtfully, "It was a great, healing light that flowed from his hands into me. I felt the warmth of it. I glowed and tingled with it.

"And then he spoke with great authority. He spoke to me. To me. 'Be clean,' he said. And I was clean. In an instant I was clean." He was silent for a long moment then, as if this were too great a thing to speak aloud.

Miriam waited, hardly breathing until he should speak again.

"When he looked at me next I thought he was angry. I knew he was angry, though his anger was not turned toward me. His eyes grew dark and stern. I felt that he was angry at the illness which had held me captive for so long. Oh, I was glad he was not angry with me. No one, I think, could withstand his anger.

"Then he said a strange thing to me. He said, 'Do not talk about this to anyone, but go to the priest and do as Moses commanded, that you may fulfill the law.'

"*Do not tell anyone*, he said. But how can I be silent? Here you are for me to tell. I have to tell it. I am alive again, and clean. And now I shall go to the priest and sacrifice for my cleansing, so that once again I may walk among men unashamed."

Then he took Miriam's hands into his own. When he looked at the left one Miriam tried not to flinch. He kissed it gently, and said, "He could heal you, you know." Suddenly he was gone, striding across the summer field.

It was only after he had gone that Miriam realized he had not told her the name of the one who had cleansed him. But she thought she knew. And she was sure he could not heal her. No one could heal her.

8

Some of the men who kept Miriam were religious, or so they said. From them Miriam learned about matters which they considered to be important, of things read and preached in their synagogues. And all the time she thought them to be the worst kind of hypocrites. *At least,* she thought, *I've never pretended to be something I am not.*

But a secret voice told her, *You are as bad as they are. You pretend to be what you are not each time a man makes love to you. And remember Nathan? Your hypocrisy began with him.*

Am I responsible for his death? she asked herself, knowing well what the answer was.

One such religious man, Jairus, an official in his synagogue, kept Miriam in a pleasant little house just outside Capernaum. The city lay at the northern end of the lake of Galilee, beside a bay. Liking the lakeside house so much, Miriam sometimes forgot to hate the man. He professed to love her more than his own life. But many men had professed the same, and in the end their lives dictated that they leave her. So she went on to the next.

Jairus bore more guilt than the others, since he was

devout. "In the synagogue," he told Miriam, "when I speak out against adultery, I want to tear my clothing and heap ashes on my head, for I am guilty. Then I think of you. I see your face, and I cannot keep myself from returning to you. You have ensnared me. I am consumed with love for you."

"But surely love is not wrong," Miriam soothed him, knowing that love had nothing to do with his feeling for her.

Jairus liked to tell Miriam about his family. His daughter was his treasure and his pet. Miriam used to envy her, just hearing Jairus speak of her so tenderly. "She is twelve years old," he told Miriam one day. "I have sons, but my daughter is like a young flower. How anything can be so lovely, I do not understand."

"What is her name?" Miriam asked, not really caring.

"We have named her Deborah for a woman who was a prophetess in ancient times. But sometimes we call her *Talitha*. Little girl."

Miriam thought that the name of a prophetess was a heavy burden to lay upon a girl. She was glad that her own name was a common one, even though it meant *Bitter*. Her name suited her.

One evening Jairus came to Miriam and his face was ashen. He walked like a man stricken with a deadly malady. When he saw Miriam he did not speak. He stood before her like one dazed or terrified.

"My love," Miriam went to him. "Are you ill?" It did not move her to see him so. She spoke merely from a sense of duty.

He sank to the floor and sat motionless as an idol.

"My love?" She sat beside him, stroking his hands. "Are you ill?" she asked again. "How may I help you?"

Finally he spoke. "Miriam, Miriam. I am punished for my sins. My Deborah is near death. Last week she was full of life, happy, singing, greeting me with a kiss. Today she is stricken and lies motionless, as if she is already dead. When she dies, her death is on my head, for it is my sin which has brought this upon her."

Miriam thought he was foolish for thinking such a thing. But she made comforting sounds and stroked his hands.

"It is my sin which is killing my child," Jairus insisted. "But here I have come to you again." He groaned. "I am a man torn, divided. I adore my child. I cannot bear to see her as she is. But I cannot bear to be without you. Help me, Miriam. Comfort me."

So Miriam comforted him, and for a while he forgot his pain. But when he left her he looked like a man who walked toward his own death.

She wanted to feel grief for Jairus, but she could not. For long years she had felt nothing except the hate and scorn which she nurtured within herself. Only since the wedding at Cana, since the day of the leper had she felt something stir within herself which was neither.

On the next day Jairus came again and this time he brought his daughter with him. Miriam was surprised to see the girl glowing with health. *Why has he brought her here?* Miriam wondered. *Surely it is foolish. Even dangerous.*

Jairus spoke to his daughter. "Deborah, this is Miriam who has asked us to take tea with her."

Miriam tried to show no surprise. She prepared tea,

minted and refreshing, and she brought honey cakes and dates to serve. She glanced at Deborah when the child was not watching. Her eyes were dark, her hair the color of ripe wheat under sun. She looked as if she had never suffered an illness in her life.

"I love honey cakes." She smiled at Miriam. "My mother is teaching me how to make them. But I don't like it when my hands get sticky." She licked her fingers with a mischievous look at her father. "May I have another?"

Miriam passed the cakes to the child. "I'm glad you like them." Then, glancing at Jairus Miriam said to the girl, "I'm sorry you were so ill. You feel better now, do you not?"

"Yes." Deborah looked down, her expression closed, as if she had a secret which she did not want to discuss.

When Deborah had finished her cakes, Jairus asked her, "Would you like to walk in the garden for a while? Or beside the lake?"

"Yes, Father." She turned to Miriam. "Thank you for the cakes." Then impulsively she added, "I love your hair. I wish mine was like yours. I wish I looked like you."

Jairus flushed. "You look like yourself, and that pleases your mother and me. I will see you later when I have spoken with Miriam for a moment." When the girl had gone he looked at Miriam without speaking.

She had a sense of change, of finality. "Please sit beside me here." They sat together. "Your daughter is very lovely. I understand why you were so worried about her."

Jairus looked at Miriam sadly. Then he said, "Even Deborah sees how beautiful you are. I wish what I must tell you now were not so, but I must say it. This is the last time we shall see each other. You may stay in the house

80

until you can make other arrangements which will please you. But I can no longer be with you."

So that she might not seem surprised or ungracious, because he still was her protector, Miriam said, "I understand. Let me tell you how happy I am that your daughter was not seriously ill. She looks a bit pale, but one can see that she has completely recovered." Miriam was silent for a moment. Then she said, "I am surprised that you brought her here, to this house. To me. What have you told her about me?"

"Only that you are a friend."

"And does she believe you?"

Jairus said quickly, "Of course. She is completely naive. Entirely pure."

"Yes, I can see that. But why have you brought her here?" Miriam insisted.

"I know the danger, the risk of it," Jairus said. "But I have brought her so that you might see for yourself what has happened."

"I do not understand."

"My daughter was dead," Jairus said. "And now she is alive."

A wave of nameless fear engulfed Miriam. It was almost as if she knew what Jairus was going to tell her. She wished she did not have to hear it.

"Let me tell you," Jairus said, "exactly what happened when I left you yesterday. There is a rabbi in the city who has been amazing people with his teaching, with his healings. He is so different from other rabbis that I am at a loss to explain him to you." Jairus spoke softly. "He healed a leper. I have seen the man with my own eyes."

I, too, Miriam thought, but she did not speak.

"Yesterday when I left you," Jairus continued, "I feared what I might find at home. Burdened with fear and my own guilt I walked slowly, as if to delay a terrible thing. Then I saw this rabbi, Jesus, about to enter the house of Matthew, the tax collector. Some of his friends were with him. I saw them all enter the house."

Miriam wondered what this had to do with Jairus' story, but she did not interrupt him to ask.

"When I arrived at my home," he continued, "it was as I had feared. My wife was heaping ashes on her head and tearing her clothes. I knew then. I knew. I found Deborah lying dead. She was white, absolutely without color, and still and cold when I bent to kiss her. I thought then that I would die myself from my own pain and guilt. But we do not die so easily, do we?"

Miriam knew the truth of that, but she did not answer.

"Then I remembered the healing of the leper." As he spoke, Jairus' voice became excited and full of wonder. "I ran from my house, leaving my dead child, my wailing wife, and all the servants in their tumult. I ran to the house of Matthew and into the presence of the guests.

"At once I approached the rabbi. How can I tell you how he seemed to me? He was serene. He looked at me as if he knew me, though I was a stranger to him. I went to him knowing that he could help my daughter, even though she were dead. I knew it. I do not know how, but I knew it.

"I spoke to him and I felt that he understood all I would say and all I could not say. 'My daughter has just died,' I told him. 'But come and touch her, and she will live again.' Then I started home without looking back.

"I sensed that he followed me. When he and his friends

82

came with me to my house we heard the musicians making the music for mourning. The professional mourners were already there, for my wife had summoned them. The din was mighty, with my wife and the servants and all the mourners wailing.

"Jesus looked at them and said, 'Leave us. The girl is not dead. She is only asleep.' They all laughed at him because they had seen that she was dead. Nevertheless, I told them to go.

"Then Jesus and his three friends stood looking down at Deborah. My wife, thinking me mad, cowered against the wall." Jairus looked at Miriam solemnly before he said, "You will think me mad, too, for what I am going to tell you now."

Miriam thought, *I will not think you mad, no matter what you tell me about him.*

"I find it hard to believe myself, although I see her as she is today. Jesus simply looked down at Deborah, and I cannot describe the love and pity I saw on his face. He took her small cold hand and said, 'Talitha, stand up.'

"In a moment she stood beside him and looked around her as if she were wakening from a dream."

Even this, Miriam thought. *He can do even this.* She would have liked to run from Jairus so that she would not need to hear any more.

"When my wife and I came to our senses, after we had kissed Deborah and welcomed her back, Jesus and his friends had gone. I did not even have time to thank him. But I will thank him, Miriam, I will thank him with my life. It was through my own sin that my daughter died. I believe that. Now it will be through my repentance that

83

she will remain alive in this new life which has been given to her."

New life, Miriam thought. *What I would give for a new life.*

"Go to Deborah now," Jairus said. "Perhaps she will tell you what she has not told me. She will not speak of this thing that has happened to her. Perhaps she remembers nothing. I do not know. But perhaps she will talk to you. She seems to be taken with you." He kissed Miriam's fingers. "And why not?"

Miriam picked a fragrant crimson rose and took it to Deborah who stood looking out at the water.

The girl took the rose and smelled it, put the soft petals against her cheek. "It looks so new," she said. "It's almost as if I'd never seen a rose before, or smelled one. Does that sound foolish?"

"No," Miriam said. "Sometimes I feel that way, too."

Deborah turned to Miriam. "Are you my father's friend?"

"Yes," Miriam told her. "A friend." But she thought in despair, *I have no friends. Not one.*

"Do you know what happened to me?" the child asked. "Did my father tell you?"

Miriam hesitated. "He told me that you had been very ill," she said finally, "and that now you are entirely well."

"Yes." Deborah touched the rose with her lips. "But there's something I haven't told them. I'm afraid they wouldn't believe me."

"I see." Miriam did not rush the child into speech. She waited.

"Will you laugh at me if I tell you something really strange?" Deborah asked.

84

"I will not laugh. I promise."

"I don't want you to tell my father. Not anyone. Promise?"

"Yes. I promise that, too."

Why is she telling me? Miriam wondered. *Why me?*

Deborah plunged into her story. "It was when I was sick, just yesterday. I felt as if I couldn't breathe and I hurt all over. And I was so cold. My mother and father were worried. I knew by the way they looked at me. And I guess I knew I was going to die."

The girl's eyes were puzzled as she spoke. "I don't know how I knew that, but I did. And then, I went someplace else. It was . . . well, it was strange. First I saw my mother standing by my bed and she was crying. And I saw my father kiss me, and he cried, too. I wanted to tell them not to cry because I was right there with them, watching." She looked at Miriam as if she were afraid Miriam would laugh at her.

But Miriam only asked, "What happened then?"

"Well, for a minute it was dark. Then it was just as if I were standing in a shower of light. It was so beautiful." She sighed. "But I couldn't stay."

"Why not?" Miriam asked.

"Because a voice told me to come back. I was sad, at first, because the new place was so beautiful. But he told me to come back, to stand up, and so I did. But he knew how I felt."

"Who?"

"The man who took my hand. I liked him. He knew how I felt. His eyes were so . . . I don't know." The girl was silent for a moment. "He was different from anybody else. I wanted him to stay with me. I wanted to be with him.

But he didn't stay. And then my parents were hugging me, and here I am." She laughed as though she were delighted at the whole incredible story. She looked at Miriam. "Isn't it wonderful?" she asked.

"Yes," Miriam said. "It is wonderful. Perhaps you will want to tell your father about it. I think he would like to know. Your mother, too."

"Do you think they would believe me?"

"Yes. I am sure they would believe you."

Jairus came out to them then. "Look, Father. See what Miriam picked for me." Deborah held out the crimson rose. "It smells so sweet. And see how beautiful it is."

He touched the rose, his fingers lingering on the petals. Looking past the flower to Miriam he said, "Yes. So very beautiful."

Miriam knew that the message in his eyes was one of farewell. When they had gone, she thought, *How much Jairus loves his daughter. I wonder what such love might be like.*

9

Miriam let it be known that she was looking for a new protector. She knew she would not have long to wait, and she wished that she could have time to sort out the feelings which had been engendered in her by Deborah's story.

How could she possibly believe that this man, this Jesus whom she had held as a newborn in her father's barn, could heal lepers and raise a child from death? Yet, how could she not believe it? And why had he looked at her as he had, at the wedding in Cana? With grief. What could he know of her life?

She was of two minds. She wanted to run from him and from his mother, and yet she longed to be near him, to see him, hear him talk.

On a day when she walked by herself, she saw a crowd gathered and she wondered whether Jesus might be there. Thinking of stones, as she often did, Miriam skirted the edge of the gathering. No one seemed to notice her. Everyone appeared to be waiting, expecting someone. Something.

And then she saw him. Jesus. Some of his friends walked with him. Men from the crowd ran to kneel at his feet. People crowded around him until Miriam could not see. She moved to a small rise, under a tree, where she could watch.

A man rushed toward Jesus, panting with exhaustion. He carried a young boy in his arms. *That boy is too big to be carried,* Miriam thought. *Why doesn't he walk by himself?*

He was a strange looking boy. His eyes were dull, his mouth wry and twisted. His body seemed anything but alert and lively.

As Miriam watched, the boy began to writhe in the man's arms. The man laid him on the ground. The boy frothed at the mouth and made animal sounds, his body twisting and turning, his heels beating on the ground, his arms and hands flailing and wild, as if they belonged to someone else, for it was apparent that he could not control them.

The man spoke to Jesus with anguish in his voice. "My son is possessed by a demon. I have asked your followers to cast it out, but they could not. Oh Master, help him. Help my son."

Jesus looked at his friends with scorn. He seemed to be angry with them. He asked, "How long do I have to put up with you? Have you learned nothing? You are faithless." His anger was frightening to watch. None of them spoke.

Then his anger abruptly changed to something else. Compassion? He asked the boy's father, "How long has he been like this?" Jesus watched as the boy writhed and foamed, as he lost control of his bladder, as the stream of urine ran along the ground under and beside him.

The father was almost weeping. "He has been this way

all his life, Teacher, for he is moon-crossed. The demon holds him and does with him whatever it will. Once it flung him into the lake. He would have drowned, but one of his brothers saw and rescued him."

The man wrung his hands. Miriam was almost touched by his anguish. "Oh Master, it was terrible. One day the demon flung him into the fire and held him, in his convulsion, until my wife saw him. He was burned so severely that he bears scars to this day. Have pity on us. Help us."

Miriam thought she would faint from the force of her own heartbeat. She hid her scarred hand deep in the folds of her clothing. She remembered the fury of the fire which had burned it. She felt the fury of the fire which still burned within her. But deep inside her, something pleaded silently with Jesus, *Help him*, though the boy and his father were nothing to her.

Once again the eyes of Jesus met Miriam's across the heads of the crowd and she saw pleading in his eyes, though why he should plead with her, she could not imagine. Then, still looking at Miriam, Jesus spoke to the father of the boy. "All things are possible to him who believes."

At once the boy's father cried out, "I believe. Help my unbelief."

You are wrong. Miriam silently challenged Jesus. *For me, nothing is possible, except what is.*

The crowd pushed closer, looking at the boy, at Jesus, murmuring to each other.

Then Jesus spoke, and his voice was stern and powerful. "You dumb and deaf spirit, I command you, come out of him and never enter him again." His hands were raised above the boy and Miriam saw brilliance all around

89

them, like flame, touching the body of the convulsing youth.

The boy writhed with one last, terrible convulsion. Then he lay still. His face was peaceful. He looked as beautiful as a marble statue, and as lifeless. Miriam could not see him breathe.

Someone in the crowd whispered, "He is dead." Soon the whole group took up the words. "He is dead. He is dead."

But Jesus bent and took the boy's hand and raised him up. The boy opened his eyes and looked around him. He was held by Jesus' hand and Miriam saw that the two looked at each other for a time as if no one else were near.

Then the boy's father embraced his son, weeping and laughing at the same time. The boy remained mute, enduring his father's embraces, but looking at Jesus over his father's shoulder. Jesus raised his hand in a kind of salute, or farewell, to the boy before he and his friends moved away.

As they moved, they passed Miriam where she stood at the edge of the crowd, under the tree. She heard one of Jesus' friends ask him, "Why could we not cast this demon out?"

Jesus' voice was sad, but no longer angry when he answered, "Because your faith was not strong enough."

Miriam was close enough to touch him, but she shrank back so that even his clothing would not touch her own. He did not look at her as he passed by, but she was sure he knew she was there.

Soon the crowd dispersed. They had seen their miracle. *They have something to talk about,* Miriam thought, *and it will last them until the next time.*

Only the boy and his father remained. Still the boy had not spoken. Miriam watched, wondering what he would say when he did speak. He leaned against his father and said, in a voice so weak that it trembled, "I am so tired." He was still very pale and Miriam could see that he was near collapse.

She spoke without thinking. "Come with me. The boy may rest until he is strong enough to walk to your home." She had not intended to speak. Her voice went its own way.

The father supported the boy, half carrying him, and they walked together to Miriam's house. To Jairus' house. Miriam invited them in and made the boy lie down. She brought fruit and tea. The lad sipped a bit of tea, but he ate nothing. The father could not eat, either, but only stared at his son with a kind of tranced wonder. Miriam had never seen her own father look that way at any of his sons. Or at his daughter.

She asked the boy, "What was it like? What did you feel when he cast the demon from you?"

The boy looked at Miriam and said, "I've lived my whole life in fear. I would lose part of my day, not knowing where the moments went. I would wake, as if I had been asleep, and my mother and father and my brothers would be looking at me with pity and I would hurt all over. Sometimes my mouth would be bleeding, for I had bitten myself. Sometimes I was wet, smelling of my own wastes. Once, when I awoke, I had been burned."

Again Miriam hid her own burned hand in her clothing as she listened to the boy.

"The worst of it was that people have always been afraid of me. They have shunned me, since I was pos-

91

sessed by a demon. No one wants to be near demons. I know that." He looked at his father sadly.

His father embraced him again and said, "My son, we have always loved and treasured you."

"I know," the boy said. "I know. But now you will not have to be ashamed of me any more. I will be like other boys."

The father wept again. "My son," he said, "You must not hope too much. The Teacher banished the demon today, but perhaps it will return. We cannot really know. It was a strong demon. Do not hope too much."

The boy held his father's hand and said quietly, "It will not return. He banished it forever. He told it never to come back, and it will not. I know it. I am sure."

"Then I will lean on you," the father said, "for your faith is stronger than my own."

When the boy was rested, they prepared to leave. The father said to Miriam, "It was a kind thing you did, to take us in. No one else thought of it. We thank you."

Miriam saw that the man knew who and what she was. And still, he thanked her. She nodded, not risking words.

Then the boy said, "I thank you too. You are so beautiful. So good."

Miriam saw a kind of worship in his eyes. His words pierced her like the knife with which she had gashed her brother, the other Jesus, those long years ago. When they had gone she sat alone, staring at the wall or past it, seeing nothing, hearing nothing but the words of the healer.

At last she covered her ears and shut her eyes, hoping to be rid of the sound and the sight. But he would not leave her.

***

Soon after the healing of the boy, a young man came to the house near the lake to ask Miriam to go with him to Jerusalem. Jerusalem was too near Bethlehem for Miriam's comfort and she told him so.

"I can give you anything you want," he told her. "I am wealthy." He did not speak as if he were boasting, only as if what he said was fact.

He was very handsome. His blond hair curled close to his head, showing small ears which were well shaped and perfect. He looked strong.

"What are you called?" Miriam asked him.

"My name is David. You do not need to know my family name," he told her pleasantly. "I hope you will come with me. I have heard many things about you. They are true. You are as beautiful as they have told me." He took her hands. When he saw the scars he did not flinch.

"That does not sicken you?" Miriam asked, her voice half-scornful, half-teasing.

He did not speak, but only touched his lips to the livid scars.

Inwardly Miriam laughed. He was so young. But she thought, *If I go with him, at least it will put distance between me and Jesus and his mother.* She asked him, "When do you go to Jerusalem?"

"In three days' time. Will you come with me?"

"I will come," Miriam told him.

"And if I cannot wait three days?" he asked, trying to embrace her.

She laughed and, with an easy gesture, pushed him away. "It is not long to wait. I will be ready for you when you come."

After he had gone, Miriam took one of her solitary walks into the countryside, near the spot where she had talked to the cleansed leper. She saw people clustered there around someone whom she could not see. As she came closer, she heard a man ask, "Who is the greatest in the kingdom of heaven?"

Miriam thought, *I know who is there, ready to answer that question.* She did not want to stay. She wanted to turn and run, but something drew her, and she walked closer, toward the voice which she knew would speak. The question puzzled her. The questioner spoke as if the kingdom of which he spoke were a real place. She knew of no such realm.

But flooding into her mind came memories of the time of the birth of Jesus. Of voices singing in the heavens, of blinding star-fire. Memories of visitors bearing gifts to a baby they called a king. Painful memories of a time she wanted to forget.

In spite of the looks of disdain, scorn, and hate which were leveled at her by some in the group of people gathered there, Miriam edged nearer so that she could see the one who would answer the question. *Who is greatest in the kingdom of heaven?*

Jesus sat on a little hillock, surrounded by people. He wore his homespun robe, and his presence was simple, serene. Vital. He looked up and Miriam was sure he saw her there, at the edge of the group. She was sure he knew her. His eyes were full of sorrow as he looked at her. He did not speak to her, but she felt as if he had called her by her name.

Jesus held out his hand to a small girl who was near him, standing beside her mother. The child came, putting her small hand into his with complete trust, leaning against him, even touching his cheek, feeling his beard.

Jesus smiled down at her, still holding her hand as she leaned against him. Looking at Miriam, he answered the question which had been asked of him. "I tell you the truth. Unless you become like a child, you will never enter the kingdom of heaven. Whoever is like this child is the greatest in the kingdom."

Again he smiled into the face of the little girl. She smiled, too, as if they shared a secret. Then he looked at Miriam once more. She saw her own face reflected in his eyes. She saw all the Miriams. Her own young self, lying up in her loft, looking at the stars, seeing the beauty of the world as it unfolded outside.

She saw her suffering childish self, filled with rage and hate.

She saw a procession of young girls behind that first dirty Egyptian child; girls whom she had grudgingly gifted.

She saw the pale face of a young boy, cleansed of his demon, as he rested in her house.

"Whoever receives one such child in my name receives me," Jesus said. He looked at Miriam with such compassion that she knew he meant that she had done this, although she did not know she had done it for his sake.

Then his eyes grew dark, his voice became stern. It was as if the bright day had suddenly clouded. Still looking at Miriam, he said, "But whoever causes one of these little ones who believes in me to sin, it would be better for him to have a great millstone fastened around his neck and to be drowned in the depth of the sea."

His eyes still held Miriam's, and they were filled with that grief she had seen in them before when he had looked at her. Sitting there, among all the people who had come to hear him, and with the child still beside him, he spoke again as if it were to Miriam alone. "Blessed are those who are persecuted for righteousness' sake, for theirs is the kingdom of heaven."

Miriam was once again thrown back into time. The time after Jesus' birth, when the Messenger had told her to warn Joseph to leave Bethlehem. The time when she had given them the donkey so that Jesus and his mother could ride away from her. The time when she had, indeed, been persecuted for his sake.

But *righteousness?* What, Miriam wondered, did that mean. Was it his other name? Did he mean that she, Miriam, could become blessed? She, who lived a life for which all the self-righteous sneered at her, and worse? And the kingdom of which he spoke. The kingdom of heaven. *I can hope for it to become mine?* Miriam thought. He had to be mad, as many said he was.

But he continued to look at Miriam as if no one else were there. She saw, in his eyes, the faces of her father, her brother, the traveler who had abused and hurt her. Those who had set her on the path which she still followed.

Miriam closed her eyes so that she would not have to look into the eyes of Jesus. Behind her own eyes she saw those men, her father, her brother, and the others, with great millstones around their necks, drowning in an angry sea, waves covering their heads, their hands groping for something, anything to cling to.

A great rush of unholy joy filled Miriam as she saw them all drowning in her imagined sea. She laughed, silently, as she saw them fighting, struggling for breath. She wanted them all to die there as she watched.

But she opened her eyes and saw Jesus watching her. He said, "You have heard that it was said to men of old, 'You shall not kill; and whoever kills shall be liable to judgment. But I say to you that every one who is angry with his brother shall be liable to judgment.'"

Miriam was filled with indignation against Jesus. Was he telling her not to be angry with her brother? The brother who had treated her so vilely that she had been changed forever from the child she once had been?

It isn't fair, she told Jesus silently, as he looked at her.

Nothing is fair, Miriam, his eyes told her. *But until you are able to forgive them all, you will not rest.*

Never, her mind told him. *I will never forgive them. Or you, either. It was for your sake that it all happened to me. I will never forgive any of you.*

Then his eyes left Miriam. He gave the child back to her mother. The little girl moved toward a clump of scarlet blossoms. She broke them off and brought the flowers on their ragged stems back to Jesus.

He took them from her and as Miriam watched, the stems became long and glistening with moisture, as if they were newly sprung from the earth. From where she stood, Miriam caught the scent of the blossoms, sweeter than anything she had ever smelled. They glowed in the sunlight, scarlet as blood against Jesus' homespun robe, the stems and leaves green with new life.

With a cry which escaped in spite of herself, Miriam turned and ran toward Jairus' house, faster and faster, until, out of breath and stumbling, she flung herself on her bed. Despair rose in her, growing until she thought she would choke on it. But she did not weep.

10

On the day Miriam and David left Capernaum for Jerusalem, he brought proud, spirited horses for them to ride. "We need not hurry on our journey," he told Miriam. "We will sleep by night in tents draped in silk, and we will feed on such delicacies as you have never tasted. You will have everything you desire."

How can he give me everything I desire, Miriam wondered, *when I do not know what it is myself?*

Miriam enjoyed riding the beautiful horse which David had provided. At first, when he had suggested that they ride, she had said, "But I have never been close to a horse. I have never ridden."

"Then I shall teach you. You will ride like a man." David had taught her, but soon she felt that she had nothing to learn. She was an extension of the proud animal, and she exulted in the feeling of being so high. She saw the earth differently from her position on the horse's back. She felt that she was born to ride.

Evenings, on the leisurely ride to Jerusalem, when she was sore from the new demands upon her muscles, Miriam would lie while David massaged her with sweet-scented oil. She began to wish that the ride to Jerusalem were longer.

She became friends with the other animals as well. The pack-donkeys reminded her of her own little donkey, and she would feed them bits of good things from time to time. David laughed at her, but tenderly. He was bewitched by her, and he was ardent and gentle. But she could not love him. She felt more for the donkeys and the horse than she did for any person and she was empty. Empty.

The house outside Jerusalem was more beautiful than any Miriam had seen. It was furnished with precious things: carpets of crimson and royal blue, carved chests and furniture, hangings of rich fabrics. They ate from plates of silver or of gold. David gave Miriam everything she asked for, and much she did not ask for as well.

He even supplied her with a serving girl named Abigail, a pleasant, soft-spoken young woman whose home was in Jerusalem.

But in spite of all his wealth, David was melancholy much of the time. "Miriam," he asked one night while they were together, "why does it never last? This feeling I have during moments of love?"

She did not tell him that for her it was not love.

"Why does nothing ever last?" His eyes were pensive, his tone sad. He was a serious and thoughtful young man and Miriam hated him less than she had hated some of the others.

"Love may not last," she told him, "but we can renew it at your pleasure."

He kissed her warmly but drew back with hesitation. He told her, "You are so beautiful. Our time together is more precious to me than anything. But you will grow

100

old. Your beauty will fade and finally you will die. Then I will grow old and follow you. Where will we be then? Life is an illusion. We cannot hold or keep it, no matter how we try."

"Do not be so sad," Miriam coaxed. "You are young, with a long life ahead. And I am not so old that I feel my own death to be near." She laughed, teasing him.

But he said, "We grasp at sunlight and it flows through our fingers. We grasp at moonlight and it vanishes, silent and silver. We grasp at dreams, and they elude us. All that I own will decay as if it had never been. Nothing lasts. Nothing."

Miriam was bewildered that her young lover was so sad. She used all her arts, and though he would lose himself in her for a time, he would again be pensive and melancholy.

Late one afternoon David came in and lay down silently upon the silken cushions. Miriam brought him minted tea. She leaned close so that he could catch her scent which always delighted him.

"Come." She sat close to him. "I have brought you tea."

He refused the tea and lay without speaking, his arms under his head. Miriam waited beside him until he chose to speak.

At last he said, "I have heard of a rabbi, newly come to Judea, who teaches strange things. He heals the sick. He casts out demons. It is whispered that he can even raise the dead. I cannot believe that. But I have seen this teacher. I have spoken with him."

Can I never escape him? Miriam thought. *Will I have to go down to Sheol before I am rid of him? Will he follow me all my life?*

"Let me tell you about him, Miriam. His name is Jesus. He travels from place to place. They say he has no home, although once he lived in Nazareth."

Yes, thought Miriam. *And he was born in a cave in Bethlehem.*

"He has friends, even though he has no home. I have seen them. Young men, like me. They are always with him."

Miriam waited for him to continue. When he remained silent she asked him, "Would you like to be his friend? Is that the trouble?"

"I think he is in danger," David said. "The priests are angry with him because he interprets the Law in ways they cannot condone. I think they will ruin him, finally. But . . . "

Miriam was afraid. "But what? Why should they care what he says or does?"

"His teaching is too radical. He threatens them. They say he does not keep the Law. But I believe he knows it better than they do."

"How do you know these things?" Miriam asked.

"Today I went to hear him where he was speaking to his friends and anyone else who wanted to listen. On a sudden impulse I asked him, 'Master, what must I do to have eternal life?' I do not know how he can make such a promise, but he does. He promises eternal life to those who follow him."

"No one can live forever," Miriam protested. "Even I know that." *Nor would I want to.* "You yourself said that life is an illusion."

"I know," David said. "I know. But if it were possible?

If there were a better life, after this one has ended? If one could win it somehow, by good deeds? Or even by magic?"

"What did he tell you?" Miriam asked.

"He said that first I must keep the Law. Well, I have kept it. I have never stolen anything. I've never needed to. I've never killed anyone. If I have enemies, my father sees to them. I have always honored my father, and I have never lied. There has been no need.

"As for committing adultery, I acknowledge my sin. But it is because I love you. And there is no sin in love." David began to laugh.

"Why do you laugh?" Miriam asked. "You have said nothing amusing." Her tone was cold.

David reached for her. "He said that I must love my neighbor as myself. Be my neighbor, sweet Miriam. Be my neighbor and let me love you as myself. And more. For I do not love myself very well."

Miriam drew away. "What else did he say? Please tell me."

"He talked about the kingdom of heaven. What it is like. He is a good story-teller, that rabbi. He said that the kingdom of heaven is like a mystery, and those who have ears can hear about it. And he said that the kingdom of heaven is like the smallest seed of all. The mustard seed. Although it is small, it grows to be the size of a tree. Or, he said, the kingdom of heaven is like leaven which works while it is hidden."

"I do not understand any of this," Miriam told him. And she saw a shadow cross his face. "Now what are you thinking of?"

"He said that the kingdom of heaven is like a merchant

103

seeking the finest pearls. When he finds a pearl of great price, he sells everything he has to buy that pearl."

"That story makes you unhappy?" Miriam was impatient. "I do not find it sad."

"No. That is not what troubles me. I asked the rabbi again what I must do, after I have observed the Law, for I would like to be his friend. He said something to me which was so strange I could not believe it."

"Tell me."

"He said that to be perfect I must sell all I have and give everything to the poor. 'Then,' he told me, 'you will have treasure in heaven. Come and follow me.'"

David took Miriam's face in his hands and kissed her eyes, her cheeks, her lips. When he released her he asked, "How can I give it all away? If I did, I would lose you."

Miriam closed her eyes. And once again the face of Jesus came into view, and she could not shut it away.

***

"I would like to take you to Greece one day," David said to Miriam. "And to the island of Crete. Have you been there?"

"You know I have not. I have told you," she said. "I've been only to Egypt. And I do not wish to return there."

"Then let me take you to Greece. Many wonders are to be seen there. Strange tales are told by the Greeks, about

104

their gods and their heroes." David stroked Miriam's hair as he talked. "Do you know the story of the Minotaur and the labyrinth?"

Miriam asked him, "What is a Minotaur? And I do not know about a labyrinth."

"I shall tell you the story." David moved away so that he could look at her as he talked. "There was once a king on the island of Crete. His name was Minos. He had a bastard son who was half man, half bull."

Miriam interrupted. "Then this is only a story? It is not true?"

David laughed. "You must decide for yourself. The king was ashamed of this son and hid him in the bowels of the palace. He had a maze constructed there, a labyrinth, he called it, so that the son would be well hidden from everyone. There, in the dreadful safety of the labyrinth beneath the palace the king fed his son the only food he craved. The flesh of young men and virgin girls." David's voice was that of one who tries to frighten willing children with stories of spirits and monsters.

Miriam shuddered. "I do not like this story. Tell me another instead."

But David insisted, "Listen. It's a good story. A hero, a prince from the mainland of Greece, came to Crete as an intended victim for the Minotaur, for that is what they called the beast. The prince found his way through the labyrinth with the help of a young priestess, and he slew the beast and freed all the young men and women who were being held captive. Would you not like to see a country which produces such fine myths? I could take you there."

"I am happy here," Miriam said, though it was not true. "I have no desire to go anywhere."

David was suddenly serious. "It might be well if I were to take you away from here for a while."

"Why?" Miriam asked. "What is wrong?"

"It is my father," he told her. "He would harm you if he could, because he hates you."

A chill touched Miriam. "Why does he hate me? He has never seen me."

"He has seen you. He has made it his business to see you. He hates you because he fears that I will waste my inheritance on you." David reached to touch her face. "It is not waste for me to be with you. You are all I care about. You know that I worship you."

Miriam stroked his hair. "You are very good to me. Your father will not harm me, surely."

"You do not know him." David's tone was stern. "He is not a man to trifle with. You would do well to be alert. I am going to see him today, to talk with him. Please stay here, Miriam. Do not leave until I return. I truly am afraid for you."

"I will miss you while you are gone," she told him, although it was not true. "And I will not leave the garden or the house."

"Abigail will be with you," David reminded her. "She will watch over you." He caught her up in his arms. "I could not bear to lose you."

When he had gone, Miriam went to the walled garden. It was one of those spring days when everything is touched with new life. Miriam sat beneath a flowering almond tree. The blossoms billowed above her. A breeze carried the scent of the flowers to her, and the humming

106

of bees. Peace was everywhere. Everywhere but in Miriam's heart.

She thought of the man-beast in the labyrinth. *I know what he looked like. He looked like my oldest brother. No wonder they hid him away. I'm glad he was finally slain.*

Then she remembered the words of Jesus about forgiving. *I doubt that Jesus has as much to forgive as I do. Surely he could not expect me to forgive what was done to me.*

Looking up, facing into the sun, Miriam saw a woman approaching her. Thinking she might call Abigail, Miriam stood. She wondered if it might be one of the wives of her lover, or his mother, come to confront her. She steeled herself.

The stranger walked toward Miriam. She was dressed in simple homespun. A white shawl covered her head and shoulders, falling in soft folds. She walked lightly, with the step of a young woman.

Then Miriam saw her face, and it was not the face of a young woman, but Miriam recognized her at once, as she had the day of the wedding in Cana. The eyes had not changed. Those eyes greeted Miriam with such clarity that she felt ready to weep. But not quite. She had not wept since she was a child. Stone women do not shed tears.

"Miriam," the visitor said. "Miriam. Dear child."

"I am not a child." Miriam spoke before she thought. "I lost my childhood soon after you left me."

"Dear child," Mary said again.

"You stole my childhood," Miriam said. "You and your son stole it from me."

Mary looked at Miriam, her eyes filled with pain. "How you have suffered."

Miriam thrust out her hand so that Mary could see the scars. "Yes. I suffered for your sake. Joseph said he thought I would have to pay for giving you the donkey. I paid when my father burned this hand in the fire. And I paid in other ways, as well. Those scars are hidden. I have been paying all my life." She felt her bitterness gather, rise, and overflow.

With a fluid motion, Mary sat on the ground under the flowering tree. She touched the ground beside her and asked, "Will you sit here with me for a while?"

Miriam sat near her. She looked into the face she had loved, at the woman who had said her name with understanding and compassion. As she looked at Mary, a sense of shame began to suffuse Miriam. She knew that she was in the presence of a pure woman, one to whom her own life would be anathema.

Miriam was glad that she was simply dressed at that moment. She wore no cosmetics, as she had at the wedding at Cana. Still, she wanted to leave the presence of this woman who was so different from herself. But the ground seemed to pull at her, and she could not stand. Then she realized that she was staring at Mary. It was as if she were being fed after a long period of starvation.

Mary took her hand, the scarred one, and held it while she talked. "I knew we would meet and talk again one day. I told you so long ago. Do you remember?"

"I remember. Were you in Egypt long? I have been there, too. I did not like crossing the desert."

"We had a safe crossing. Your little donkey served us

well. When it was time, we went to Nazareth. My son grew up there."

Miriam felt as if she would choke on the name. "Jesus. I have seen him. I have seen him cure . . . " But she could not talk about him any more.

"Yes. He does wonderful things." Mary looked steadily at Miriam. "Let me tell you about his boyhood. My husband, Joseph, was a carpenter, you know, and he taught Jesus his trade. Even as a little boy, my son's hands were deft in handling the tools: the adz, the chisel, the saw. He seemed to love the wood he touched, smooth planks of cedar and cypress. Even then his hands were different from the hands of others." Mary was silent, lost in her remembering.

"How did he become a rabbi?" Miriam asked.

"He was a diligent student," Mary told her. "He learned the Law and the Prophets early, as the boys in our villages do. But one day, when he was twelve, we took him to Jerusalem with us. A strange thing happened there."

Miriam thought, *I do not want to hear this. Not any of it. What are they to me?* But she listened.

Mary continued, "He became separated from us. We looked for him for three days. I was frantic. We finally found him in the temple talking with the teachers and the wise old men. I saw him there. I watched them listen to him, saw them look as if they were amazed by what he said.

"But I was frightened at having lost him, and I was impatient. I asked him, 'Why have you done this to us?'

"He answered me, 'Did you not know that I would be here, doing my father's work?' He was not insolent when

109

he spoke to me, only calm. His authority was unmistakable. And he was only twelve years old. 'I would be here, doing my father's work.' "

Miriam was puzzled. "His father's work in the temple? But his father is a carpenter, you said."

Mary spoke so softly that Miriam had to lean toward her to hear. "Do you not yet know who his father really is?"

Miriam stared at her. Here was a woman as chaste as any woman could be. Miriam knew that. Although she was neither pure nor chaste herself, she recognized these qualities in others. And Mary was telling her that Joseph was not the father of Jesus?

Mary seemed to know what was in Miriam's mind. She said serenely, as if she were telling the location of the sun when it rises in the east, "Miriam, Jesus is the son of God."

Is she mad? Miriam wondered. But Mary was serene as the garden itself. Her eyes met Miriam's with candor and peace. Miriam remembered the events of the birth of Jesus, and the events which followed. Singing stars, voices from the sky, and the visit of magi with precious gifts. And she thought of the Messenger.

"I know it is hard to accept this thing," Mary said. "You may be thinking of the angel who came to you in your dream. It was the same Messenger who came to me when I was a young girl with the news that I would bear God's son."

"You saw the Messenger?" Miriam asked her.

"Yes. He came to me one evening when I was alone. I was so young. Not yet sixteen. I had been daydreaming.

Of Joseph. And suddenly the air stirred and I knew I was no longer alone."

Miriam knew she was breaking a spell but she said, "You saw him. You really saw him? What did he look like?" Her own memory seemed to come from another life. She, too, had been a child, innocent and chaste, when the Messenger had come to her, a lifetime ago.

"I saw him clearly," Mary answered. "He was light itself. The room vibrated with his light. His face was so bright that I had to close my eyes against its shining. And his wings were great, living sweeps of radiance. I was afraid."

"I was afraid, too," Miriam told her, "and I only dreamed him. What did he say to you?"

Although she was a woman well past her fortieth year, Mary looked like the young girl she had been as she answered. "He said, 'Hail, Mary, full of grace, the Lord is with you.' I was terrified. He knew it and he told me not to be afraid. Then he told me that I would bear a son, even though I had not been with any man. And he told me that my child would be the son of God." She shook her head as if to clear it of unreality. "It was a hard thing for so young a girl to accept. You can imagine how it would be."

"And Joseph? How did he feel?" Miriam asked. "And your parents? And the neighbors?"

"I think that at first Joseph would have liked to break our betrothal. In the end he came to believe and accept as I did. Still, it was a hard time for all of us."

Miriam sighed. "But your parents loved you? They did not cast you out?"

"No. They loved and nurtured me." She looked closely at Miriam. "You were not so fortunate, were you?"

111

"No."

"You were the first to see my son, after Joseph and I had seen him. Do you remember?"

"I remember." Miriam knew she could never forget. Then she asked Mary, "What if you had told the Messenger no? What then?"

Mary spoke with childlike simplicity. "But one does not say no to God."

Miriam suddenly realized what it was that made Mary different from other women. She was obedient, even to messages she did not understand. When she heard a heavenly message, she had obeyed it.

Again Mary seemed to be reading Miriam's thoughts. "You were obedient, Miriam. You were obedient, even knowing that your obedience would cause you pain. Now the time is nearing when my son must be fully obedient, too, knowing that his obedience will bring him pain." Mary looked at Miriam as though she were puzzled. "I do not know how I know. But I do. I am afraid for him. Terribly afraid."

"Can't he leave here and go somewhere else?" Miriam asked her. "I have heard that he is in danger from the authorities. He could just leave, couldn't he?"

Mary only sighed. "What he must do, he will do. No matter what it costs him." Then she looked at Miriam almost sternly and urged, "Do not resist him. He can help you. I know that you are bitterly unhappy. Listen to my son. He can help you." She rose, shaking white blossoms from her skirt.

Miriam stood too. *She looks so young,* she thought. *As if she will never grow old. I am not worthy to be here with her. I wish she would let me go.*

112

Mary touched Miriam's face. "Deep within you is a beauty to match the beauty of your face and your body. I know it is there. God bless you, my Miriam."

She left the garden as quietly as she had come. The emptiness she left behind her was so stark that Miriam was desolate. That emptiness was a symbol of her own life as she had lived it. She saw Mary's virtue beside her own wretchedness, and she knew complete despair.

She looked at her maimed hand. *Mary is wrong. Inside, I am as ugly as this hand. Sheol waits for me. I belong in the kingdom of the lost.*

If her knife had been nearby, Miriam would have used it on herself at that moment. She would not really be taking her life, she felt, because she was already dead. She had not the energy to walk, but she leaned against the tree, hardly able to stand.

Abigail came into the garden and found her there. "My lady," she said, alarmed, "are you ill? Come, let me help you." She led Miriam to her bedroom and helped her lie down. She covered her with a light coverlet. "May I bring you tea?" she asked.

But Miriam could not answer. She lay prone, staring at nothing. Abigail sat beside her while dusk gathered. The day ended and stars glittered in the heavens. Night birds began their songs. Fragrance from the garden floated through the air. Life and beauty flourished. Only Miriam, in her misery, felt herself to be without life, exiled from all beauty.

11

When David returned to Miriam in the house outside Jerusalem, she was too anguished to welcome him as she always did. She was weary and did not desire to be with him. But she knew that she did not have the strength to resist him or to refuse him.

He did not wish to be with her. He was bemused. Late in the afternoon he began to tell her his story. He talked all through the night. From time to time he sipped wine, but he did not eat.

"My love," he began, and his voice was sad.

Miriam knew at once that he would leave her. She could always tell when the time had come for parting. She was not sorry, and she was not glad. She could feel nothing except the emptiness which she had felt since Mary had visited her—the emptiness which she had known most of her life.

"My love," David said, "this is our final time together. My family plans to harm you and I must leave you so that you may be safe. I hope it is not already too late. My father is powerful, as I have told you, and he swears he will not rest until he has ruined you. You must leave this place."

Miriam took his hand and tried to soothe him. "Do not be afraid for me. I will leave this house, of course. I will be safe. In any case, I have had a longing for the sea. I will go away, and you must not be concerned for my welfare."

Miriam knew of a man who wished to become her protector. He lived in Jerusalem in the upper town, and had made his desire known to her through an emissary. But she did not think it necessary to tell David that.

David kissed her hands. "You do not know my father. He will follow you. He vows to destroy you. I hope I can prevent him. I have promised him that I will return to my home in the city and be a dutiful son and husband. Perhaps that will be enough for him. Even now I know it will not be enough for me. Not since you have shared my heart."

Once again Miriam said, "Do not be afraid for me. I will be safe." Bitterly she thought, *I have never shared anyone's heart. Not since I was a child and shared my own heart with Mary.*

He said, "There is another thing I wish to tell you. The telling of it will be long, for much has happened. I wish to tell you before we part."

Miriam settled near him on a purple cushion, assuming an attitude of deep attention. "Tell me, then." It was easy to please him and it was her duty, since she was still in his house.

He asked, "Do you remember what I told you of that rabbi who said I must sell all I had and follow him?"

Miriam shuddered inwardly, knowing well of whom he spoke and not wishing to hear more. She said only, "I remember."

"Jesus." David's voice caressed the name. "I heard him

once again when I was near the lake, in Galilee. I followed him, although once before I had turned away from him. He and his friends walked up into the hills a long distance. I followed with the crowds.

"I have never seen so many people in one place. It seemed to me that there were thousands, following him into the hills. Men, old and young, women, children, babies in their mothers' arms. I saw all kinds of people. The rich, the poor. The lame and the healthy. The road was clogged with them. The grasses of the field were crushed under too many heels. Thousands of people."

Miriam asked, "And were you alone, in all that crowd?"

"No. I took my nephew with me. My brother's son, Daniel. He is a merry boy, and good company. He had a packet of food with him." David smiled. "He is always hungry. He is a handsome lad and has not yet attained his full growth. How he can eat!

"We followed with the rest. Daniel had cut a whistle from a reed and he piped as we walked. The sun was warm. A hot wind had risen and overnight the flowers had bloomed; scarlet anemones, yellow daisies, creamy lupin. The fields were alive with color. The lake far below us sparkled in the light. It was a beautiful day. Perhaps it was the wind which made me uneasy, but my heart was heavy, in spite of all the beauty, knowing, even then, that I would lose you." He buried his face in his hands.

Miriam stroked his hair and absently murmured love words until he lifted his head and spoke again.

"Daniel somehow managed to edge toward the front of the crowd and we stood quite near Jesus and his friends.

117

The rabbi looked as I have always seen him look. Calm, untroubled, dressed in his homespun robe and sandals.

"You would have thought it impossible, outdoors and among all those people, that he could be heard. But everyone was still, when he began to speak. Even the children were quiet, resting against their mothers or playing with the flowers and the grass, or listening. Something in that man compels one to look at him, to listen to him. I cannot explain it. He is like no one I have ever met."

Miriam wanted to say, *I know. I know.* But she did not speak.

"A man in the crowd called out, 'Master, teach us. Tell us what we must do.' " David shook his head in wonder. "The things he said in answer were so strange. Miriam, you will not believe the things he said."

"Tell me," she urged, knowing that he wanted to tell her, even though she did not want to hear. She wanted nothing to do with that man who looked at her as if he knew her, as if he grieved over her.

"When he stood there, he made me think of Moses, speaking from the holy mountain, long ago when he brought the Law. Jesus is like another prophet who brings a new Law." David spoke solemnly.

Miriam remembered Nathan as he tried to explain the Law to her and to Esther, his wife, in Bethlehem. She thrust the memory from her.

David said, "The first thing that the Teacher said cut me to the heart. He said, 'Happy are you who are poor, for yours is the kingdom of God.'

"He said that to me before, do you remember? I told you. He said I must sell all I have and follow him. I cannot do that. My great wealth is my responsibility and my joy.
118

Once I told you I could not give up my wealth because then I would lose you. Now I am going to lose you and still I cannot give it up. Wealth is power. I intend to use it. But . . ."

Miriam thought Jesus had said a strange thing. She had never considered poverty to be desirable and she knew it did not bring happiness. Her parents had always been poor. She had determined never to be poor herself. And she was not. She had amassed valuable possessions, and she intended to keep them. Now here was Jesus saying that the poor would inherit a kingdom. She was confused.

David continued, "He said, 'Happy are you who are hungry now, for you will be satisfied.' My nephew looked at me with merriment in his eyes, and tapped his bundle of food. I had to smile at him. But I had the feeling that it was not only of bread that this teacher spoke.

"I looked around me at the people who were listening to him. Many of them were gaunt and pale from constant lack of food. They stared at Jesus as if they were being fed, just listening to him.

"And he said, 'Happy are you who weep now, and are sad, for you will be filled with joy.' I saw faces which were lined with old sorrows, and they were filled with new hope. Oh, Miriam, if I could only tell you what it was really like, that day."

Miriam had felt no joy, all the years of her life, and she had not wept, either. *Perhaps, if I could weep?* she thought. *But weeping is for the weak. Or for those who can hope.* She was too full of despair and pain to allow herself to weep.

"I can't remember everything he said," David told her.

"But one other thing remains in my mind. He said, 'Whatever you wish that men would do to you, do so to them. Love your enemies, do good to those who hate you, bless those who curse you, pray for those who abuse you.' I remember those words just as he spoke them.

"Can you even imagine those things? My father says that if one is harmed or abused, it must be an eye for an eye. Full vengeance. I do not know what kind of vengeance he plans for you, but it makes me afraid. But what could the rabbi mean? I wish it could all be so, what he says. But do you think it ever could be? People are not like that, are they? The people I know are not."

"I do not know," Miriam answered. "Such things are far beyond me." She spoke ritually so that he would not be uncomfortable, thinking that a woman could know more than himself. But secretly she believed that Jesus could not be right.

Surely he could not think that she, Miriam, must forgive those who had made her life what it was? How could she ever forgive her parents, her oldest brother, that traveler who had forced her, when she was a child? She looked at her ruined hand, thought of her ruined life and recalled that she had sworn to curse all those who had harmed her. She knew that she would never cease to curse them all.

Jesus was a dreamer. One might wish things like that to be true, but men were not like that. Or women either. Men had always crushed and destroyed those weaker than themselves, and Miriam had no reason to think they would ever change.

David broke in upon her thoughts. "I do not know how long Jesus spoke. He appears to be a mild man, but when
120

he speaks, one must listen. He has authority, but I do not know where he gets it."

Mary herself, his own mother, had marveled at her son's authority, when he was only twelve. And Miriam could not forget the magi with their gifts, and the horrors which King Herod had visited upon Bethlehem, out of fear of Jesus, newly born. These things all spoke of a mystery which Miriam could not understand.

"The people on the hillside listened," David told her, "as if he brought them something they had waited for all their lives. I felt that way myself. Then, in the middle of a pause, I heard my stomach rumble, telling me that I was hungry. Daniel laughed, and so did those around me, in sympathy. I was close enough to Jesus and his friends to hear what they said to each other then. They talked about food.

" 'How shall we feed them?' one of the young men asked Jesus. 'They are so many, and most have brought no food with them.'

"I heard Jesus say, 'Tell them to sit down.'

"The young man lifted his arms and called out to the people, 'Please sit down on the grass. Be comfortable for a while.' Some people were already seated. I sat on the ground beside Daniel. He uncovered his bundle, looking at the bread he had brought, and the few dried fish. They smelled so good that I could feel the juices rising in my mouth.

"Then I saw that Jesus looked at Daniel. He did not speak, but he looked at the boy, a long, clear glance. Before I could stop him, Daniel stood and took his packet to Jesus. Jesus smiled at him, a smile that could break

121

your heart with its sweetness. Daniel came back to sit beside me on the grass. Neither of us spoke to the other.

"As I watched, Jesus took the bread from Daniel's bundle and lifted it high and blessed it. He broke it into pieces and some of his friends began to pass it among the people sitting nearby. The Teacher did the same with the few, spicy fish. He blessed them and then he broke them and they, too, were passed among the people.

"Daniel and I were given bread and fish. I have never tasted anything so good. That bread was like . . . I cannot think of any bread like it. It was sweet, and fresh and fragrant. The fish was pungent and delicate at the same time, and we ate our bits of bread and fish, and we were filled. My hunger has never been so easily satisfied with so little.

"All those people feasted on Daniel's loaves and fishes, and each one was satisfied." David shook his head in disbelief.

Miriam thought of the wine she had tasted at the wedding in Cana, of its delicate, exotic flavor. She had never again tasted such a wine. It seemed to her that everything Jesus touched became transformed.

"When everyone had eaten," David said, "the friends of the rabbi moved among the people, and when they came back to Jesus I saw that the baskets they carried were full of bread and fish. It could not have happened, but I saw it.

"All the way down the hill Daniel did not talk to me. He only piped a little tune on his reed flute. It was too strange a thing to talk about. I have spoken with others since then, others who stayed longer than we did. They told me that Jesus healed a blind man that day. A man who had been blind since his birth. He cast out demons from another, a man who had always been demon-possessed. I did not see these things. But somehow, I do not doubt them."

Miriam felt an aching in her throat. She knew it was more than bread and fish which Jesus had given to the multitude that day. What it was, she could not explain, not even to herself. But she was sure that there was none for her. She had been hungry all her life. She felt that she deserved nothing more. She would have liked to weep with misery. But she had no tears.

When David finished talking, it was dawn. He had talked away the night. He took Miriam's face between his hands and kissed her eyes, her brow, her hair. He did not kiss her lips. Tears stood in his eyes as he said, "Good-bye, my Miriam. We will not meet again. The best thing I can do for you is to leave you. Go from this house as quickly as you can. Go where you will be safe."

He went so suddenly that she did not have time to answer him, although what she might have said, she did not know. He was a kind young man, but he meant nothing to her.

Once again she was alone with her pain. She was outside the circle of Mary and Jesus and their friends. Her life had put her outside their radius. There was no hope for her. She was alone. Empty. Lost.

12

Micah looked at Miriam, his face, as always, an enigma. "Tonight," he told her, "we attend a dinner at the home of Simon, a client of mine. He is both wealthy and influential, for he is much respected in his circle of religious men. He is a leader. I am honored that he has invited me, and he has permitted me to bring a guest. I wish you to accompany me."

This new protector of Miriam's was older than most of her lovers had been. He was a man of wealth, earned through his own efforts. He dealt in luxurious wares: rugs and hangings, bronze lamps, fabrics rich beyond description.

The house in the upper town into which he had brought Miriam was full of treasures. She found that she missed a garden, the lake, the sense of nature close at hand. She disliked the feeling of being enclosed. But she had no choice.

"My lady," Abigail often said to her, "you are sad. What is it you want?"

Miriam would look at the girl whose clear brown eyes questioned her, and she could not answer.

"Can I bring you something?" Abigail often asked. "Tea? Honey cakes?"

But Miriam could not be eased of the burden which lay heavy upon her. The feeling of heaviness. The prevailing sense of her dislike of herself.

Micah was generous in his gifts to her. He brought her jewelry fashioned of gold and of pearls. It was far different from the gaudy beads worn by many of the Hebrew women. And he brought her gifts of wonderful fabrics, shot through with gold or silver thread. He had garments made for her from them, robes which revealed more of her flesh than she would like to have revealed. But he only laughed when she objected.

He gave her as many denarii as she asked, and more. But a subtle cruelty was evident in his manner. It became increasingly difficult for Miriam to be the willing and enthusiastic partner he demanded in the many ways of love which he wished to practice.

Miriam saw her life stretch ahead endlessly in the pattern she had established for herself. She longed for the energy, the will, the opportunity either to change her life or to end it.

Now she faced Micah and asked him, "Is it wise, my lord, for you to take me with you into the house of one of your clients?"

He was silent, and his tight, secretive smile made her uneasy.

"I am pleased, of course," she told him, "to be in your presence. But is this wise? Can it harm you in any way?"

He laughed, a sardonic sound which chilled her. "Harm me? I have no secrets. All Jerusalem knows of our alliance. Everyone knows how fortunate I am." His lean,

126

handsome face was turned toward her and she caught the glint of latent violence in his dark eyes. Still, she was not actually afraid of him because she knew that she pleased him.

"Thank you, my lord," she said. "I have not meant to imply that you have anything to fear. I know your courage and your importance."

"It is of no consequence," he said. "I know that you mean me no disrespect. It gives me pleasure to display you. Of all my possessions, you are the most precious, the most beautiful."

Miriam bent her head. "Thank you, my lord." *His possession,* she thought. *That is what I am. Only a possession. A piece of fine merchandise.* A wave of self-loathing washed over her and for a moment she was dizzy and faint.

Micah did not appear to notice. "Wear your new gown," he said. "The one of silk embroidered with gold thread. And wear this with it." He held out a chain of golden links. Each link was separated from the next with a gem: a ruby, a sapphire, an emerald. It was truly magnificent.

Miriam kissed his hand. "You are good to me. It is the most beautiful ornament I have ever seen."

"Yes." He touched her. "And it is to adorn the greatest beauty I have ever known. Now make yourself enticing and alluring to do me honor. Use the Egyptian cosmetics which please me and the antimony to enhance your eyes. And wear no veil. Let your hair fall free." He stroked her hair. "No one has more lovely hair than yours, Miriam. It is pure, living gold."

She tried not to shudder as he touched her. *What is*

127

happening to me? she thought. *I am afraid. Why should I be afraid?*

"I shall take a gift to our host, and so must you," Micah told her. "Choose something worthy of a fine gentleman." Miriam heard a faint scoffing in his tone. She knew that he in no way felt inferior to the men who were his clients. He went among them with his silken manner, making them feel important. But Miriam was sure that he felt superior to all of them. She knew he was a complex man and she admired him in a way, at the same time that she was repelled by him.

Abigail helped her dress in the white silk gown which was embroidered in intricate golden patterns. Miriam held the heavy hair up from her neck while the servant girl fastened the clasp of the necklace. "It is very beautiful, my lady," she said to Miriam. "Does it make you happy?"

"I do not know what happiness is," Miriam told her. But she remembered a time, long ago, when she had been happy at the touch of a baby's fingers curling around her own. At the sight of a woman's smile. At the sound of her own name spoken by a loving voice.

Abigail held a mirror for Miriam so that she could see herself. Micah had brought it to her from some distant place. He said the women of Rome used them. Her reflection in the uneven metal surface showed her a woman whose eyes were rimmed in black and elongated in the Egyptian style. The carmined lips were full, the cheeks pale. Micah liked her pallor. The red-gold hair rippled around her shoulders. She could find no gray strands in it. *How is it that I remain so young in my appearance,* she wondered, *when I feel older than death itself?*

As a gift for the host Miriam selected a small vase of alabaster which she had purchased for herself. It was filled with a sweet ointment, costly and rare. The vase was the white alabaster which she most admired, showing faint lines of silver-gray upon its surface, the lid cunningly hinged with a golden clasp.

She took the vase with her when she went to meet Micah and showed it to him. "Is this a fitting gift?" she asked. "I would wish to honor him so that I do not dishonor you."

Micah took it from her and turned it in his hands. Handing it back to her he said, "It would honor a king." Again she was aware of the scoffing in his tone.

"What gift are you taking him?" she asked.

He showed her a small box made of precious metal, etched with scenes which made Miriam gasp when she studied them. "It will be a success if it amazes even you," Micah laughed. "Our host has unusual tastes, and I am sure this will delight him."

When they arrived at the home of Simon, their host, Micah and Miriam were admitted by a servant and ushered into a dwelling more princely than any Miriam had ever even imagined. A fountain played in the entrance hall, the water changing color as light from torches played upon it.

Miriam was startled to see peacocks walking in the hall, spreading their tails like huge, dramatic fans embroidered with eyes of blue and gold. In a corner, enclosed in a large metal cage, a leopard paced. Miriam shivered at the thought of so much strength, such potential danger restrained in so small a space.

They were led into the room where the guests were

129

assembled. The conversation stopped abruptly as Miriam and Micah stood in the doorway together, caught in a sudden silence.

Miriam looked around her. Everywhere her eyes met those of another she found contempt and scorn. In some eyes she saw lust, in others, hatred. She was the only woman in the room. Waves of violent emotion surged toward her, palpable and destructive, almost overwhelming her.

A man who looked prosperous and imposing came toward them. Micah said to him, "Simon, here is the companion I have promised to bring for your pleasure and for the pleasure of any of your guests who wish to share her. Her name is Miriam."

Simon looked at her appraisingly, with haughty scorn. "Of course. How generous of you to bring her, to offer to share her. She is well known among us. To some more so than to others."

Sly laughter rippled in the room. Miriam stood holding the vase of alabaster, feeling as though she had been changed into an alabaster woman. *Micah has tricked me,* she thought.

Then, standing among the guests she saw David, her former young lover, and in his eyes, horror. He stood beside a man who had to be his father, so strong was the resemblance between them. And in the father's eyes, as they looked into Miriam's, the most livid menace she had encountered since the look in her own father's eyes when she was a child.

She did not know what to do. Micah's hand was on her arm, clutching it in a painful grip. Miriam felt a kinship with the leopard in the next room, a prisoner in his cage, at the mercy of others.

And then. And then, as she looked about her, vainly hoping, a pair of eyes met hers and she was caught in them. The eyes spoke to her in messages so clear that she might have heard them.

Do not be afraid, my child, the eyes told her. *I am here. You are my own, as you have been from the beginning. I have come to help you, to save you, to bring you peace. I have come to name you. I name you Miriam.*

Her heart began to pound. She wanted to drown in those eyes, in their kindness and compassion. But she could not move.

Only ask me, the eyes told her, *and I will give you the new life you so deeply desire. Only ask me, and I will forgive you everything. Come to me. Come to me now, and we will walk together into your new life. Miriam. Come.*

Drawn by those eyes, by that silent voice which spoke only to her, Miriam walked toward him with no volition of her own. The crowd parted as she moved toward him, down miles of marble floor, past beasts who were eager to devour her, past the scoffers who hated her because of their own self-righteousness. She walked, as if she walked down all the paths of her life, until she stood before Jesus. Still his eyes held her.

She knelt before him, and the marble floor was cool and smooth. In that moment, all the interior stone, all the fire of her hatred's power began to disintegrate and her tears were freed.

Miriam's tears began to flow and she could not stop them. For her whole life she had held them back, forbid-

131

den them to fall. Now, free as rain, cleansing and pure, they flowed.

She felt love wash over her. His love for her, and hers for him. Love as simple as that she had felt for him when he was born. She kissed his feet.

Miriam opened the alabaster vase which she still held in her cold hands. She began to anoint his feet with the perfumed ointment. She stroked them, moistening them with the ointment and with her tears. She thought of nothing, no one but him.

Then she began to dry his feet with her hair. But her tears fell as if they would never stop. And so she remained, it seemed to her, for a lifetime, moistening his feet, kissing them, drying them with her hair.

She heard Simon speak, as if to himself. "If this man were a prophet, he would have known what sort of woman this is who is touching him, for she is a sinner."

Jesus said to him, "Simon, I have something to say to you. A certain creditor had two debtors; one owed five hundred denarii and the other fifty. When they could not pay, he forgave them both. Now which of them will love him more?"

Simon appeared to think a while and then he said, "I suppose it would be the one to whom he forgave more."

Jesus said, "Of course. You are right."

Then Miriam felt Jesus touch her head. He said to Simon, "Do you see this woman? I entered your house and you gave me no water for my feet, but she has wet my feet with her tears and wiped them with her hair. You gave me no welcoming kiss, but she has not ceased to kiss my feet. You did not anoint me with oil, but she has anointed my feet with ointment. Therefore I tell you, her sins,

132

which are many, are forgiven, for she has loved much; but he who is forgiven little, loves little."

Miriam could not stop crying. *He is wrong about me,* she thought, *when he says that I have loved much. Until now I have not loved at all, not since his infancy. Can it be that the early love has survived, in spite of everything?*

His hand still touching her head, Jesus said to her, "Your sins are forgiven. Your faith has saved you. Go in peace."

Then Miriam heard a petulant voice ask Jesus, "Why has she done this? She could have given you the alabaster jar and the ointment, for they are costly. We could have sold them and given the money to the poor."

The man spoke as if Miriam were not there, as if she could not hear what was said. *He is erasing me,* she thought. Then she heard Jesus say, "The poor are always with us. I will not always be with you. This woman's gift is precious, for she anoints me for my burial."

Miriam's heart grew heavy with anguish at his words. She saw in her memory the one who had brought him a gift of myrrh. He had said, "Balthazar brings myrrh to honor his dying, when the time comes for his death." Now Jesus spoke of his own burial. Had she, Miriam, through the evils of her own life, somehow brought him closer to his death?

How can I bear it? she thought. *Just when I have found him, I will lose him again. I know that I will lose him.*

Still weeping, she rose, lowering her face so that no one could see it. Leaving the vase beside Jesus, she slowly walked the long way back to the entrance and then she left that house. She began to run. Her face was wet. She knew it must be streaked with the cosmetic she had used.

133

Her hair was wet from her tears, and tangled. She ran toward Micah's house. She had no place else to go, although she was determined to find a place.

She ran alone in the dark night, through the maze of narrow streets, hoping she would not lose her way. She saw watch fires on the towers. The east wind blew, carrying with it the scent of smoke from the altars of sacrifice. She caught the reek of burning flesh, the odor of incense. Stumbling, terrified, she ran through the night until she found Micah's house.

She went to the sleeping chamber. She removed the heavy necklace and placed it on Micah's table. Then she removed her silken garment, now sodden and stained, and laid it with the necklace. She cleaned her face and put on her most simple gown.

She gathered the things she had brought with her when she came to Micah, her jewels, her gold and silver coins. Her hands trembled as she put them in the woven bag which she used for traveling. She knew that wherever she went she would need those things as barter for food and lodging. Micah's gifts and the clothing he had given her she would not use again.

Exhausted, she sat on a cushion, not knowing what to do, where to go. She knew that she would never again willingly lie with any man. She did not know where she could go at night, in a hostile city, alone. She only knew that she must leave.

"Go in peace," Jesus had said. But where? If she could find Mary, perhaps she would be safe. "Go in peace." Miriam was a stranger to peace. How could she hope to find it now?

As Miriam sat alone and bewildered, Abigail came in

134

to her. "Are you ill, my lady?" She sounded surprised and concerned. "I did not hear you come in. Is the master with you?"

"No. I am alone. I am not ill, only tired. Tired to death." Miriam rubbed her temples, trying to ease the throbbing in her head.

"Let me help you prepare for the night. May I bring you wine? Or tea?"

"No," Miriam told her, "nothing. Only, do you think that . . . "

"What is it?" Abigail's genuine concern comforted Miriam. "How may I help you?"

"I must leave this house," Miriam told her. "Could you find me a place to stay, somewhere in the city? A small inn, perhaps, where I could be safe for a while. Or a room in someone's home? Do you think there might be a place for me somewhere?" Miriam tried to control the tremor in her voice.

Abigail looked thoughtful. "I will try. Shall I go now?"

"Yes. And come back to me as soon as you have found a place." On impulse Miriam handed the serving girl the woven bag which contained her jewels and money. "Take this with you and keep it safe for me. I trust you."

Abigail took the bag. "Something is wrong, my lady? And you cannot tell me what it is?"

Miriam nodded. She pressed her knees together to stop their trembling.

"I understand. I shall return as soon as I can. I am sure I can find you shelter somewhere."

Still feeling too spent to move, Miriam sat staring at nothing. She thought of the words spoken to her in silence, of the touch of a forgiving hand on her head. She

135

knew that in an instant her life had changed. She did not understand it, but she knew it.

Then Micah raged into the room and the atmosphere was filled with his anger. Terror seized Miriam, for that anger was directed at her, in all its violence.

He pulled her up, holding her away from him, gripping her shoulders so tightly that she knew they would be bruised.

His words were hissing and sharp in her face. "You have humiliated me." He shook her. His breath against her face was hot. "I took you into the house of my most important client, for his pleasure and at his request, and you made a fool of yourself and of me. You have cheated me." He hit her across the face. "I own you. You have no life of your own as long as you belong to me."

Miriam was terrified as he stormed at her. She was sure that he was not telling her everything. Something more lay behind his wrath. She felt that it must have something to do with the father of David, but she could not ask him.

He threw her down and once again she was thrust back into her childhood with her oldest brother and the traveler forcing themselves upon her. The old nightmare returned. But now Miriam knew that she wanted a new life and she could not escape to look for it. Again and again Micah forced her, inflicting new and intense pain until finally she lost consciousness.

When she awoke it was morning and Micah lay beside her, one arm flung heavily across her body. She could not move without awakening him. She wondered whether Abigail had returned and left again. She could not think clearly, torn between the pain in her body and her mind's anguish.

Then Micah awoke and once again he took her roughly, brutally. All these years she had chosen her own path. Now she was helpless. She wanted to change. Jesus had named her as his own, but she belonged only to this sordid life which she had chosen for herself. She was not a woman, like other women. She was only an object to be used. She had no value.

Micah forced himself on her once again; her efforts to resist were in vain. When Simon entered the room, Miriam looked up at him, powerless to move. He was followed into the room by several other men, one of them the father of David.

Micah looked at them over his shoulder. The sound of his malicious laugh frightened Miriam. "I have been waiting for you," he said. "But I have not been idle. Now she is yours." He lifted himself from her almost indolently.

Miriam lay, paralyzed with fear, staring up at the men. Once again she saw the look in the eyes of David's father, and in that look she read death.

So be it, she thought. *This is the end toward which I have been traveling all my life. I chose this moment the day I seduced Nathan and caused his death.* But even in that moment of resignation, Miriam thought of Jesus with longing and desperate hope.

David's father pulled her up. She was glad that Micah had not stripped her, for she knew that they would have dragged her naked through the streets if they had found her so. The father of the man who had been her lover took

137

her by the hair, as her own father had done, and threw her to the floor.

"Kiss my feet." His tone was insolent. "Adulteress, ruiner of men. You have destroyed the life of my son. You kissed the feet of that crazy rabbi in the home of my friend, Simon. Now kiss my feet." He forced her face down upon his feet. Then, pulling her up by her long hair, he pushed her forward and said to the others, "Come. Let us take her out."

Like an animal, Miriam was goaded, pushed, pulled along the streets, a crowd gathering behind her. She was weak with terror and humiliation. She tried to picture the face of Jesus and his voice. *Have mercy,* she thought, *Help me. Have mercy.*

They forced her into the portico of the temple, with the crowd gathered around, eager for a stoning, and with the stones ready. She knew with helpless certainty that this had all been planned.

She looked at the stones. Most were large rocks, heavy, with jagged edges. She could almost feel their impact against her flesh. She could imagine them striking her bare feet, crushing them. She could feel one hit her face, shattering the bones, blinding her. She could taste the blood in her mouth. She hoped it would be a swift death.

Then she saw him. Jesus. They threw her down at his feet. She lay motionless, not looking up at him, only feeling his eyes on her, feeling the power of his presence.

Simon, who had been last night's host, spoke to Jesus. "Rabbi, this woman has been caught in the act of adultery. Now the Law of Moses commands us to stone such. What do you say about her?"

In spite of the danger, with a kind of detachment,

Miriam realized that nothing was said about the fact that Micah, too, was taken in the act of adultery. What, she wondered, even as she was about to lose her life, did the Law of Moses say about one such as he? Or any other man?

Jesus did not speak. *He is not going to help me,* Miriam thought. In that moment she lost all hope. She was alone, after all, and her life was really at its end. She was to make the final payment. She gazed into the pit of Sheol, alone at the last as she had been for so long. As she gazed into the darkness, she found herself hoping that the Egyptians had been wrong. She hoped that there would not be another life waiting for her. She was ready for the dark.

Then Jesus leaned forward and wrote with his finger on the ground. Miriam did not know what he wrote, for she could not read. But whatever it was, it silenced Simon. Silence lay, a heavy pause, all around her. She looked at the faint line of writing before her in the dust, and wondered what it said.

Again Simon began to speak, but this time David's father interrupted him. "That is all very well. Still, she has been taken in the very act, and the Law gives us the right to put her to death in the old way. What do you say to this? Or are you afraid to speak?" His tone was challenging and insulting.

Miriam, her eyes still on the ground, felt a hand on her head. She knew whose hand it was. He said, "Let him who is without sin among you be the first to cast a stone at her." Again he bent to write on the ground.

Through the tangle of her hair, Miriam looked up into

his face. It was stern, stern and commanding as he looked slowly about him into the face of each man there.

Miriam saw them begin to edge away from her. One by one they left, and the crowd, cheated of its amusement, began to dissipate. Miriam was left alone with Jesus. With Jesus and the heap of stones.

He helped her stand. "Look around you." His voice was loving and tinged with a faint, teasing surprise. "Where are they? Has no one condemned you?"

"No one, Lord." Miriam's vision of Sheol vanished, and her life became her own again. Silently she offered it to him, whatever was left of it.

He said, "Neither do I condemn you. Now go and do not sin again."

Miriam and Jesus looked at each other. She did not have to tell him that this last time her adultery had not been voluntary. Micah had taken her against her will, and her body was bruised and bleeding with the force of his taking. Jesus knew all of that, she was sure. He knew everything. And still he forgave her. Still he trusted, believed, chose her.

For a while they stood together there. Then he left her standing alone by the heap of stones. She watched him go. She picked up the smallest stone. It fit the cup of her hand. Its edges were rounded, the lines in it etched clean and definite. She thought it must have been added to the others by mistake, for it looked harmless.

As Miriam held the stone, cool and solid in her hand, she knew that the inner stone, annealed in her youth, had dissolved, and it was Jesus who had set her free. For a moment she held the smooth pebble against her cheek.

Abigail found her standing there and hurried toward

140

her. "Come, my lady. I have found a place for you. I returned last night, but it was not possible to speak to you then. Let us go before those men come back, though now I believe that they will not dare to harm you."

Miriam walked beside her, trusting, asking no questions.

"I am taking you home with me," Abigail told her. "I have never told you this. My family and I are friends of the mother of Jesus. She has been staying with us for a while, here in Jerusalem. I am taking you home to her and to my mother."

"I know her," Miriam said. "I know Mary." Miriam had never thought of Abigail as a person with a family and a life of her own. She had been merely a servant, a faithful, devoted servant, and Miriam had not questioned her devotion. She had only accepted it.

"Mary has told us," Abigail said. "She asked me to bring you to her now. You will be safe with us, if anyone is safe."

"What do you mean?"

Abigail led Miriam swiftly along the crowded, narrow streets. Miriam tried not to breathe in the foul odors which assailed her. She was nearly fainting with exhaustion.

"Jesus is in great danger," Abigail said, as they hurried along together. "He has disturbed the temple authorities with his words and his deeds. They are terribly angry with him because they say he interprets the Law in his own way and with an authority which he claims. They look for ways to entrap him. Today, with you, was one of their traps."

Even now, Miriam thought, *even now he is in danger*

because of me. Despair touched her, but it was not for herself.

Abigail, out of breath, said, "That is not all. They say he threatens Rome. He has more followers now, you know, all the time. He is powerful in ways none of us understand. We who know him love and trust him. His mother worries about him, fears for him."

Miriam remembered Mary's words, the day in the walled garden. "I know," she said.

"They are going to return to Bethany and stay for a while," Abigail told her. "His mother and some of their friends will try to persuade him not to return to Jerusalem. He is in such danger here."

Only Abigail's mother was at home in the house near the western hill to welcome them when they arrived. "Welcome to our house," she said to Miriam. "You will be safe with us. You must rest now, while you recover from your ordeal. I have been told what has happened. We will shelter you for a while."

It was hard for Miriam to speak to her. She had not met this kind of woman in so long a time. Not since Mary. She asked, "Is Mary here with you?"

"No. It was necessary for her to leave earlier than she had planned. But she asked me to greet you and assure you that you two will meet again soon. Now Abigail will take you up to the guest quarters and you must rest."

Miriam felt embarrassed. "You are very kind," she said awkwardly.

"Rest now. Soon we will let you share in the work, for we feed and tend others here."

Miriam went with Abigail to the roof where mats were placed for sleeping. The street noises were less deafening up here. She could hear doves cooing somewhere, and she thought she smelled the pungent odors of herbs and flowers. Beside one of the mats was her traveling bag.

"I brought it here last night," Abigail explained. "Now do you think you can sleep for a while?"

"I will try." As Abigail turned to leave, Miriam called to her. "Abigail?"

"Yes, my lady?"

"You must not call me that any more."

"What shall I call you, then?"

"My name is Miriam."

Abigail smiled shyly and said, "Rest now, Miriam."

When she had gone, Miriam lay down and closed her eyes. She tried to blot out visions of angry, vicious faces and a pile of stones. She sighed deeply, feeling new as a newborn infant, and just about as strong.

13

Miriam lost all sense of time, there in the home of Abigail and her parents. She was exhausted in body and spirit. For hours she would lie on the mat up on the roof, unable to feel, to think or to act. She could only cling to the knowledge that her life was changed. It was no longer her own, for she owed it to Jesus. But what he wanted her to do with it, she did not know.

Abigail and her mother nurtured Miriam as if she were a child, coaxing her to eat, trying to cheer her. Even Abigail's father was kind to her, permitting, even welcoming her into his household, although Miriam was sure that he knew what she had been.

People came and went in the house, often sleeping on mats on the roof, as Miriam did. When at last Miriam felt that she had the strength to try to help Abigail, she felt clumsy and inadequate. One morning Abigail was showing Miriam how to crush herbs. The scent of mint clung to her fingers and Miriam thought it was a pleasant fragrance, more pungent and clean than precious oils.

Three people entered the room, two women and a man. Abigail greeted them warmly. "It is good to see you. Have you come from Bethany?"

"Yes," one of the women answered, "we have come from home. We must speak with your mother."

"Come with me." Abigail turned to go. Then she said, "Miriam, these are our friends, Mary, Martha, and Lazarus. They are friends of Jesus."

The three women hurried away, leaving Miriam with the man. She felt uneasy. She did not know how to speak to a man, now that she had decided not to speak in the old ways.

Lazarus was very quiet. He walked slowly, as if he had forgotten how to move. His face was serene, but Miriam thought it was something more than that. It seemed oddly locked, as though all he felt and thought, all he remembered, lay behind a mask. It was a kind face, gentle, in no way menacing.

He picked up a sprig of mint and turned it between his fingers, touching, smelling it. He asked, "Do you know Jesus?"

"Yes."

For a long time he was silent, turning the mint in his hand, looking at it, tasting it. Miriam thought he seemed to take great satisfaction in its texture, flavor, and aroma.

"We have known him a long time, my sisters and I."

Miriam waited. Lazarus seemed caught in a reverie and she did not wish to break into his thoughts.

"I died, you know."

Miriam caught a touch of wonder in his tone.

"I died," he said again.

Still she waited, not knowing what to say. But she thought of Deborah, the daughter of Jairus.

Looking at Miriam, Lazarus said, "You are beautiful.

This mint is beautiful. Everything is new and bright and lovely. Still . . . "

Miriam had caught no hint of seduction in his voice when he mentioned her beauty. It seemed to her that he considered her an object to be admired, like an herb or a flower. She was puzzled. She asked him, "You died, you say?"

He looked at her, but she felt that he was not seeing her. She studied his face. It was smooth, unlined, young, although she thought he was not as young as he appeared. He looked as if he were divided in his mind. *Divided*, she thought, *between two worlds.*

"Yes," he said, "I died. But he called me back. Jesus called me back. His voice followed me, and when he called my name I had to come back. *Lazarus*, he said. I had to come back. My sisters wanted me. I think he did, too. They say he cried. So he called me, and I had to come."

Miriam doubted nothing that he said. "What was it like?" she asked him, remembering the things Deborah had told her.

"I can't remember," he told her sadly. "Not any of it. At first I did, or I thought I did. But now I can't remember. I only know that here everything seems new." Then he asked Miriam, "Did you die?"

"No. Not in the way you did. But he saved my life."

Lazarus nodded.

Miriam thought that he understood, even the things she did not say.

"He is in danger," the young man said. "My sisters and I wanted him to stay in Bethany with us, but I think he is coming back here, to Jerusalem." He dropped the sprig of mint, as if he no longer had the strength to hold even

147

so small a thing. "We will lose him," he said, so softly that Miriam could hardly hear what he said. "I know it. We will lose him."

When the others entered the room Abigail was saying, "I am afraid for him. He is not safe in the city."

"Nevertheless," her mother said, "we knew he would return. He is committed to his work among us. Let us go and welcome him. Miriam, do you want to come with us?"

"Yes." Miriam did not want to see Jesus walk toward danger. But she wanted to see him. As a deer is drawn to a water-hole, or a starving person toward bread, she was drawn to him. He fed her in a way she had never known. She did not need to speak to him, to touch him. Only to be near him, so that she could feel whole.

The four women and Lazarus went out into the street. Miriam followed, pulling her shawl well around her face so that no one might recognize her, by any remote chance. People were gathered in the narrow street, crowding against each other. Some of them held branches of palm trees. Children waved their branches in the air, poking and tickling each other with them.

Then a murmur arose. "He is coming. I see him. He is coming."

Miriam tried to see over the heads of people in front of her. She saw, in the distance, a white-robed man riding on a donkey. As he came nearer she recognized Jesus: Jesus riding on a donkey.

Tears rose in Miriam's throat as she thought of the years so far away when his mother had ridden away on a donkey, taking him out of her life. Now he came riding into it again, on the back of just such a little beast as she had provided for them.

148

Miriam wondered whether a child had given Jesus this donkey, or if the child's father had offered it. And in that moment she knew that she would again offer her father's donkey, just as she had before, even knowing the price she would have to pay. *I would do it freely,* she thought. *Freely.*

As Jesus approached, the people began to cry out and wave the branches they held. It was only a small gathering, only a small parade, Jesus and a few of his friends walking beside him. Those who recognized Jesus greeted him. Some became so excited that they took off their cloaks and threw them before him so that the donkey walked on a carpet of clothing and branches, for they threw those down as well.

Jesus rode into Jerusalem as a hero. "Hosanna," some in the crowd shouted. "Blessed is he who comes in the name of the Lord." The children cried "Hosanna" louder than the rest.

Looking around her, Miriam thought she saw some of the men who had come to Micah's house that terrible morning. "Look," she said to Abigail, "I am sure they are here to spy on him. See. Don't you recognize them?" But she could no longer find them.

Abigail said, "They will think of something. Something to use as a trap to catch him. And if they can't find something, they will manufacture it. That is what my father says."

Then Jesus rode very near to the place where Miriam stood. She saw his face clearly. He was not smiling. His face was serene as he looked into the eyes of people who watched and called to him. He reached to touch a child whose mother held him out.

149

And then his eyes met Miriam's, only for an instant. But once again they spoke to her silently, a message of trust and love. Then, as she watched, he rode out of her sight.

As if it had been planned, Miriam and the others followed Jesus to the temple. Only a few of the crowd went that far with him. But the children went, and some of the others. Jesus stepped down to touch them. Miriam remembered that he had touched her, too, in forgiveness.

The outer court of the temple was, as always, full of the tables of the merchants who sold birds and animals for the sacrifices. It was like a market, with the merchants trying to outsell each other, each loudly proclaiming that his pigeons, his lambs were better than his neighbor's. Miriam hated the noise, but most of all she hated the smells of the place.

As she watched, Miriam saw Jesus stride toward the tables. She could see that he was angry, truly angry. She hurried so that she could see him more closely and hear what he said.

In a rage, he tipped over some of the tables as if they were children's toys, spilling the money, bewildering the money-changers. Doves fluttered and called, kids and lambs bleated, children laughed and chased the animals, hitting at them with palm branches.

Miriam saw Jesus lashing about him with ropes, twisted into a whip. *Where did he get them?* she wondered. *Perhaps they were lying on the tables.* Whoever was in the way must have felt the sting of the lashing. Miriam was amazed at his anger. Amazed and frightened.

"What is he doing?" a man in the crowd shouted.

150

"These people have their licenses. Who does he think he is to come into this sacred place and cause havoc?"

Cries of outrage, the sounds of frantic animals, the shouts of the crowd and the laughter of children mingled in utter confusion.

Then Miriam heard Jesus cry out in a voice filled with anger, "You must not turn my father's house into a market."

She saw one of the elders of the temple face Jesus and challenge him. "What sign can you show us as authority for your action?" he asked, his voice shaking with indignation.

"Destroy this temple," Jesus told him, "and in three days I will raise it again."

The man was incredulous. "It has taken forty-six years to build this temple," he scoffed. "Are you going to raise it again in three days?"

Miriam heard derisive laughter, but Jesus did not answer. He only stared at his questioner.

Abigail's mother said, "Now they will be infuriated with him. They will use this against him, too. I am sure they will."

Miriam followed the others as they left the temple, looking back over her shoulder to catch a glimpse of Jesus, but she could no longer see him. As they walked away she heard the children singing again, "Hosanna. Hosanna to the Son of David." Deep within her she was afraid. And she heard, in her memory, the voice of Jesus saying calmly, in the house of Simon, "She anoints me for my burial."

***

Four days later Abigail's father came into the house carrying a jar of water. He said to his wife, "We are to prepare the upper chamber for Jesus and twelve of his friends who wish to eat the Passover meal together. They have asked for the safety of our house."

Miriam did not know much about the ceremony of Passover, so she did not understand all that was done in preparation for it. She saw that unleavened bread had been baked and wine was provided. What else was done, she did not know.

That evening the men arrived swiftly and silently, a few at a time, entering the upper room by the outside staircase. Miriam was aware of tension in the house. It had been there, mingled with a pervasive fear, all the while she had been a guest. But these feelings had intensified since the day Jesus rode into the city like a hero, to the shouts of the people; the day when he had overturned the tables of the money-changers in the temple. Those who loved him were in terror for his life, hoping that he would not risk returning to Jerusalem.

And now he was in this house, in the upper room. The women had not seen him come, but they knew he was there. A subtle change in the atmosphere told Miriam that he was there. She could not explain it, but she was sure.

The others, gathered together in that house, also shared a meal, but without speaking. Something about the quality of the silence above them pressed upon them and silenced them as well. They were uneasy, restless. Miriam sought comfort in the eyes of Abigail and of her parents.

Much later, when Jesus and his friends left, they were so quiet that no one heard them go. But Miriam knew, by a certain shifting of the air around them, that Jesus was gone, and his friends with him.

It is always that way with Jesus, Miriam thought. *When he is present, a difference is present. When he is absent, an emptiness is there which can be filled only by his presence.*

The night had not changed. The house itself had not changed. Only the very air spoke of Jesus' absence.

Later Mary, the mother of Jesus, arrived and three women were with her. Abigail's mother greeted them. "Have you eaten?" she asked. "Your son and his friends have had their meal and they have gone, but we do not know where."

"I have no need of food tonight," Mary said. "Only of a place to wait." Then, seeing Miriam, she went to her, took her hand and said, "Miriam, you must meet my friends. Here is Joanna, and here are two other Marys."

The women nodded to her, their faces solemn.

The mother of Jesus said, "Joanna is the wife of Chuza who is Herod's house-steward." She put her hand lightly on the arm of one of the other women. "This is Mary, the mother of my son's friend, James. And this," she touched the cheek of the third woman, "is Mary of Magdala."

Miriam was especially drawn to that third Mary. *She could have been my daughter,* she thought. *Our coloring is the same, and our hair. But she is in no other way like*

153

me. She has found peace. A peace which I have never known.

Then Mary, the mother of Jesus, stood before Miriam. She cupped Miriam's face with her cool, gentle hands. "Miriam, dear child," she said, "the circle is closing. We shared the beginning. We were brought together by more than the stars. Now we will share the ending. I am sure of it."

Miriam could not speak. She could only look at Mary, the pain in her own eyes answering the pain in the eyes of Jesus' mother.

As the women waited together, Mary was the still point for the others, her hands clasped lightly, her eyes closed. She was their source of strength although she had more to lose than any of them.

She is praying, Miriam thought. *I wish I knew how to pray.*

When Abigail's father arrived he said breathlessly, "They have arrested him. He and his friends were together peacefully in a garden and they came and arrested him. They have taken him before Caiaphas, the high priest. They say that next they will take him before the governor. Before Pilate."

Mary said nothing but she stood and started toward the door. The others followed, walking silently together toward a nameless Something which they all knew awaited them. It was the middle of the darkest night, the prelude to the darkest day. Perhaps it was not really dark, since it was near the time of the full moon, but it seemed to Miriam that darkness covered her, the others, everything.

Miriam walked beside the mother of Jesus. A few others gathered with them, only a few. They walked to the house of the governor and waited there. As more people began to arrive, Miriam recognized some of the men. She saw the father of David, who had tried to have her stoned. She saw Simon and others of the religious community gathered in that courtyard.

Torches threw wavering light on the faces of those men. To Miriam they looked like the faces of beasts. Evil itself was present in that place, and Miriam trembled with the knowledge of it.

Finally, toward dawn, she saw them on the balcony above. Miriam saw soldiers, their faces impassive, their posture rigid. Slowly the governor himself came out, and with him the man they had bound.

Soldiers roughly shoved him forward. He stumbled. A centurion jerked him upright and he stood, his hands bound in front of him, facing the group of people below.

Pilate looked at him. Jesus silently returned the look. It seemed to Miriam that they looked at each other forever, without moving, without speaking.

The approaching dawn was still and clear. Miriam could hear everything that was said. Pilate asked Jesus, "Are you the King of the Jews?" His harsh tone was alive with a crude kind of bewildered amusement.

Jesus sounded unafraid as he answered, "You have said so."

At his words some of the people cried out, as if they were a chorus, well rehearsed in their parts. They shouted accusations against Jesus. The sounds were the sounds of rage. Miriam's heart began to pound. She felt a hand take her own, and it was the mother of Jesus who touched her.

155

Pilate asked Jesus, "Do you not hear how many things they testify against you?"

Jesus only looked at him without answering.

Then Pilate faced the crowd again. They began to cry out once more, as if someone had given them a direction. Their crying was like a chant, and they stamped their feet as if to keep the time, raising their fists and screaming, "Release our prisoner to us. Release our prisoner to us."

Miriam had heard of the custom by which a prisoner was released at that time of year, at Passover time. Her heart lifted and she began to hope. *Perhaps they will show mercy after all,* she thought. *Where are the lepers he cleansed? Where are the deaf, the blind, the lame he has healed? Why do they not come forward to ask that Jesus be spared?*

Pilate asked, "Shall I release to you this Jesus, King of the Jews?"

And they cried out, "No. Release to us Barabbas. Release Jesus called Barabbas. Release Barabbas."

Miriam gasped as though she had been struck. A chilling wave passed over her body and she began to tremble so that she could hardly stand. It was Mary who steadied her, who held her hand tightly in her own.

I must not faint, Miriam thought. *I must not.*

In the midst of her anguish, Miriam heard Pilate's next question. "What shall I do with Jesus, King of the Jews?"

"Crucify him. Crucify him."

Miriam heard the words ring out for centuries, knowing she would never be able to forget them. She watched that bound figure standing patiently before his accusers, before those who sentenced him.

Then the soldiers brought out another man and the

156

crowd screamed in a frenzy. They called his name over and over and he stood there grinning, raising his arms and shaking his fists in a sort of salute. He was the very parody of a hero.

The crowd chanted, "Barabbas. Barabbas. Barabbas."

Miriam saw his face, leering, disfigured with the scar she had put there so long ago. Her brother, Jesus Barabbas, criminal, murderer. Her brother to be freed from a prison where he belonged, from a fate he deserved, so that Jesus, son of Mary, would be executed.

The old nightmare overcame Miriam and for a time she knew nothing more. She had reached the labyrinth in the maze of her own life and she looked upon the face of the monster.

14

When the soldiers had led Jesus away from the balcony of Pilate's praetorium and the crowd began to disperse, Abigail's mother asked Mary, "Do you wish to return to my home now?"

Mary said, "I shall wait here and follow wherever they lead him. I hope that you will wait, too." She turned to Miriam. "Will you stay with me?"

"You want me?" Miriam was astonished.

"Yes. I have told you so. The circle closes and we two will witness the end together as we witnessed the beginning."

Miriam felt that each word was bled from Mary, that she spoke above the pain. She was pale and her hand was icy as it touched Miriam. But she was firm and steady in her determination.

Miriam felt that she would die of shame and grief. She did not know whether Mary would be able to forgive her for being the sister of the man who would go free so that Mary's son would die.

"I must tell you something," Miriam said to Mary, her voice faltering. "The prisoner they have released, the murderer, Jesus Barabbas?"

"Yes," Mary said. "It is said that he is a man who has stirred up trouble, a revolutionary as well as a murderer. Do you know something more about him?"

Miriam forced herself to say the words. "He is my brother, my eldest brother." She could say nothing more.

Mary looked at her with pity. "My dear child. You have feared him from the beginning. I remember."

"But don't you understand?" Miriam looked at Mary in despair. "My brother, who is evil incarnate, will go free so that your son, who is good, may die. How can you forgive me for being his sister? How can you want me near you?"

Mary took both of Miriam's hands into her own cold ones. She looked into Miriam's eyes with such love and compassion that Miriam could not keep her tears back. She began to sob. She did not understand how Mary could be kind to her. She only knew that her brother would be free while Jesus would die the agonizing, humiliating death of a common criminal.

Perhaps, Miriam thought, *I will finally have the courage to use the knife against myself. Not in the home of Abigail. Her family has been kind to me. But later, in some hidden place, alone. I will offer myself as a sacrifice to show my repentance. But to whom? To what?*

That day was a small eternity. Mary, Miriam, several of the other women, and finally John, a close friend of Jesus, lived out the hours together. Those hours unfolded in Miriam's mind like a great banner on which was depicted scene after scene of a drama. The banner unfurled and covered all the earth and sky. It was lit by a sun which burned itself out behind clouds which grew more and more dense.

160

Miriam would have liked to turn away so that she would not need to be caught in the suffering. But she forced herself to watch, to be a part of the drama as it played itself out before her.

***

She sees herself watching. She is a spectator but she is also a participant, for she is suffering as each word, each action is branded on her mind and in her heart.

What they have done to him inside the praetorium, she does not know. But when they lead him out and she sees him again he is wearing the crude mockery of a crown. It has been fashioned like a cap and pressed down upon his head. It is laced through with great thorns which pierce his head and his brow. Blood runs down his face.

Miriam thinks fiercely, *I hope the ones who made it, who put it on him, stabbed their hands with those thorns. I hope their wounds never heal.*

Jesus carries on his shoulders the crossbeam of wood which they will affix to the standing beam when they arrive at the place of execution. He staggers under the weight of it. Miriam sees blood seeping through the back of his white robe.

They have whipped him, Miriam thinks. *And they used the Roman whips. Micah told me about them. He thought it was a matter of amusement, the invention of such a*

161

thing. The whips are tipped with metal barbs which tear the flesh.

Jesus stumbles. The soldiers roughly pull him to his feet and steady him. He takes a few more faltering steps before he falls to the ground, the wooden beam lying across his body.

One of the soldiers seizes a man near Jesus in the crowd of watchers. He is a large, powerful man, with shoulders that look broad enough to carry a full-grown tree. He looks terrified.

"Pick it up, ' the soldier commands him, pointing to the crossbeam. "Carry it."

The man picks up the beam as if it were an infant branch. Miriam sees the looks which pass between the two men, Jesus and the one who is forced to carry his burden.

It is as if Jesus says, *Thank you, my friend, my brother.*

And the stranger says, in spite of himself, *I'm sorry, friend. Let me help. I'm strong enough.*

The soldiers laugh and joke together, prodding Jesus as if he is an animal led to the sacrificial slaughter.

Miriam is crying. Many of the other women weep, too.

Jesus speaks to the weeping women. "Daughters of Jerusalem, do not weep for me, but weep for yourselves and for your children."

Miriam does not hear the rest of his words because she is caught up in the pain which she sees in his eyes. She is near enough to be able to touch him. She knows he suffers from the pain of his many wounds. But it is more than that. Miriam feels sure that she has somehow made his suffering greater by the pattern of her own life.

The walk is long. The people follow the narrow, twisting Jerusalem streets. Some of the bystanders mock Jesus. Miriam wonders how many of them had called *Hosanna* when he rode into the city only a few days ago.

A man spits at Jesus, the spittle falling on his cheek. Jesus does not react. A woman reaches out to wipe his bloody, tormented face with her veil.

Another man slaps Jesus in the face as he passes by. Mary flinches. John, the friend of Jesus, steps up beside her and for the rest of the eternity of that day he is with her, at her side.

Miriam has almost failed to notice that two other men are also carrying their crossbeams. The people who see them cry out, "Thieves! Thieves!"

The two men curse and the soldiers lash out at them. They groan and strain as they carry their loads to the hill outside the city. The hill looks like a skull, if one uses imagination. It is called Golgotha.

When they have reached the hill outside the city wall Miriam loses sight of Jesus. People she does not know press against her. She struggles to see him. Then she realizes that they have forced him to lie down upon the ground. She hears the hammer blows as the spikes are driven into his flesh.

Miriam hears Mary gasp with each blow as if she feels them herself. John steadies her. Miriam hears screams as the other men are nailed to their crosses. She covers her ears with her hands.

Finally she sees three crosses standing against the darkening sky. Jesus hangs on the center one, a thief on each side. Miriam looks at them and closes her eyes. It is too horrible to watch. But she forces herself to open her eyes, to watch Jesus. It is the least thing that she can do.

163

They have taken his white robe from him and he is exposed and nearly naked on the cross. The soldiers use the robe as a prize and cast lots for it. Some of them look up at the man suffering above them. He is just another criminal.

One soldier calls to him, "King of the Jews, if you are a real king, come down off your throne. Save yourself." The others laugh at this as if it is a huge joke.

Miriam sees that an inscription has been placed above his head on the cross. She cannot read so she does not know what it says. But she hears others reading it, laughing. "This is Jesus, King of the Jews," they mock.

Miriam thinks of the three who brought gifts to his birthplace in Bethlehem. She wonders where those three are. Dead, perhaps, for they were very old then. And what would they think of the fate of the child they called a king?

Mary, John, and a few of the others move closer to the cross so that Jesus will know they are there, that they have not left him to die alone. Miriam follows. She does not know whether Jesus sees them.

Her heart is filled with searing rage. She would like to be able to kill the ones who have done this to him, all of them.

Almost as if he has heard her thoughts, Jesus says aloud, "Father, forgive them. They do not know what they are doing."

Forgive them? He asks his father to forgive the men who are doing this to him? Miriam thinks of her own father, of her oldest brother, of everyone who has hurt her. Forgive them? She can scarcely breathe for the pain and fury which engulf her.

As the crowd rails and jeers at Jesus, slowly dying, one of the thieves shouts back at them. "Hold your tongues. This man has done nothing wrong. Scream at us. We deserve our fates."

The other thief curses at the one who has spoken. The first twists his head so that he can look at Jesus. Miriam is sure that he speaks out of great agony of body, but with a different kind of pain as well. "Jesus," he says, "remember me when you come into your kingdom."

Jesus answers him, "I tell you the truth. This very day you will be with me in Paradise."

A thief in Paradise? Where is Paradise? Miriam wonders. If it is where Jesus will go, is there hope that she can go there, too? She can scarcely wait until she can plunge the knife into her own breast, if that is what it takes to be with him.

The hours extend themselves to an eternity. Sometimes, during that eternity, Jesus looks down and sees those whom he knows, gathered near him. Miriam is sure that he sees, with those pain-glazed eyes.

Miriam sees him look at his mother. She believes that he sends a silent message to her, one which only Mary can read. Then he says to her, "Woman, behold your son." His eyes go to John, his friend. He says, "Behold your mother."

Mary leans against John and his arm encircles her. She is close to fainting as she watches her son die. Miriam thinks of the birthing time. She remembers the hurt marks on Mary's face then. And she remembers the fingers of a newborn curling around her own, and his first smile. She remembers the soft baby flesh. Mary must remember all that, and more.

165

She hears Jesus say, "I am thirsty."

One of the soldiers dips a sponge into a container of liquid, places the sponge on a long rod, and reaches it up to Jesus' lips.

A man Miriam once knew told her that a soldier dying of his wounds is so thirsty that all he can think of is water. Here is Jesus dying, Jesus who by his presence alone knew how to quench every thirst.

Miriam watches everything, hears everything. The sky grows dark, although night has not come. She hears Jesus cry out, with amazing strength and power, "My God, my God, why have you forsaken me?"

Mary whispers, "Why are you so far from helping me, from the words of my groaning?"

Miriam thinks that these words must have a special meaning for Mary and her son, although she herself does not recognize them.

Miriam sees that some of the elders of the temple have gathered here to watch their enemy die. David's father is among them.

One of the priests looks up at Jesus and says, "You said you would destroy the temple and raise it up again in three days. Now save yourself." His tone is scornful and mocking. "If you are the Son of God, come down from the cross."

Jesus does not answer. Miriam wishes those men into Sheol along with the others who are responsible for this death. She wishes them a death like his, or worse.

At last Jesus groans, and the sound comes from the very depth of him. He says, "It is finished." His head falls forward.

He is dead. The drama is ended. The lights of the world

166

have grown faint, the clouds deepen, the earth seems alien, forbidding. Miriam thinks she feels the ground shake. Everything is over for Jesus.

The thieves are still alive. Soldiers break their legs with clubs so that they will die more quickly. The men scream, but faintly, as if they have no more strength.

Miriam no longer cares to live in a world where such things can happen. It is a world of horror, of unspeakable ugliness. She wants no further part in it. If there is a God, and if he is the father of Jesus, how can he let such things happen? And to his own son?

She is determined to remove herself from such a world as soon as she can.

One of the soldiers sees that Jesus is already dead. They do not break his legs, but they pierce his side with a spear. Miriam sees blood pour from the wound.

The crowd begins to disperse. The spectacle has ended. The source of their amusement is dead. They go home to wait until the next public execution.

Mary goes to the foot of the cross where her dead son hangs. She embraces his feet, torn by the nails which have held him there. His blood drips down upon her and she does not notice. John gently tries to take her away. She will not go. Her friends stay near her.

Although the drama is finished, the day is not yet over. Miriam does not know how long they remain by the cross. But at last a man comes, one whom John calls Joseph. A Joseph was present at Jesus' birth. Now a second Joseph attends his death. A friend named Nicodemus has come with this other Joseph.

The Romans have given his friends permission to take the body.

167

The men take down the body of Jesus from his cross, bearing his weight in their arms. Mary kisses the still, pale face, the wounded hands. They take the crown of thorns from his head.

They wrap him in a shroud which one of the men has brought. Nicodemus carries a heavy bag full of spices with which to prepare the body for burial.

Miriam remembers the night when she anointed his feet with precious oil and with her tears. Now she knows what he meant when he told Simon, *She anoints me for my burial.* He will finally be wrapped in cloth and in fragrant spices: aloes, frankincense, and myrrh. Will Mary want to use the gifts which the magi brought to his birth? For his death?

Joseph must be a wealthy man, for he has offered a new tomb which is in a garden. Miriam walks with the others to the garden, the men carrying the body of their friend. She watches while Jesus is laid there. Joseph and the other men place a large stone before the mouth of the tomb.

Mary is so exhausted that she can barely stand. John half-carries her as they all leave the garden. Miriam wonders where he will take her, but it is not a time to ask. Even so, Mary looks at Miriam before they part, and Miriam knows it is farewell.

She walks with Abigail and her mother to their home. No one speaks during the long walk. Miriam goes to the guest chamber on the roof and lies on her mat. She tries not to see the things which she has been watching this day, but they rise before her. She lies awake all through the night, alone.

The one who might have saved her is gone.

When morning comes she will leave this house and go somewhere, anywhere, to a hidden place. Then she will, by her own hand, leave this life where evil has the last word.

15

Lying awake on her mat in the upper room all that night, Miriam was aware of comings and goings below. *Perhaps people are gathering here,* she thought, *to try to console each other.* She did not want to see anyone, to speak to anyone. She only wanted to make an end to the life which she found unbearable, now that Jesus was gone.

She slept toward morning and awakened when Abigail spoke to her. "Miriam?"

Miriam's eyes felt heavy, full of sand. Her body was weary beyond words. "Yes, Abigail?"

"I am sorry to disturb you, but my father has news from the city and we thought you would like to hear it, too."

"Of course. Thank you." She dressed and, taking her bag of coins and jewels, went down to the room where the family had gathered. Others were there as well, people she did not know and some whom she had seen with Jesus. Faces were pale and strained. She thought these people must have been as sleepless as she had been.

Abigail's father said, "I have been to the temple and I have hard things to tell you. Some of the Pharisees went to Pilate after Jesus was laid in Joseph's tomb. They

171

demanded that the governor place a guard at the tomb so that none of us who love him can steal his body. Now armed soldiers guard the tomb. They will not let him rest even after they have killed him."

"Will they prevent us from preparing his body with the spices Nicodemus provided?" his wife asked him. "We have planned to go to the tomb tomorrow."

"I do not think they can prevent you, but they may watch you."

What does any of it matter? Miriam asked herself. *He is gone. Everything is over. I must leave this place where they have been good to me. I can only harm them by my presence if I stay. The only good I can do anyone is to remove myself from the earth.*

When Abigail and her mother went to prepare the morning meal, Miriam followed them. "I must leave now," she told them. "I thank you for all your kindness to me."

"But where will you go?" Abigail asked. "Please stay with us. Here you are among friends."

"You are welcome to stay," Abigail's mother said.

"I am grateful, but I am going to be with other friends," Miriam lied, "and I will be safe."

Abigail asked hesitantly, "You are not going back to . . . ?"

"No," Miriam assured her, "I am not going back to him. I am going to people who expect me."

Miriam felt that they did not believe her, but they did not try to stop her. She offered a gold coin to Abigail's mother. "Please use it to help others as you have helped me," she said.

Abigail embraced her. "Be careful," she said. "And come back if you can."

"Thank you," Miriam said. "I will." But she knew she would not.

"Go in peace," Abigail said.

Without really thinking where she would go, she walked in the direction of Bethlehem. As she left the city she glanced toward the hill where only yesterday three crosses had stood. The crossbeams were gone, the uprights standing empty. With their usual efficiency the Romans had cleared the space for the next executions, whenever they might be.

Miriam walked the few miles to Bethlehem not noticing anything along the way, shielding her face from dust with her shawl. She spoke to no one and she hoped no one would speak to her. Almost in a stupor she walked to Bethlehem, the place of her birth. And his. She expected nothing, hoped for nothing.

In a matter of hours she arrived. She passed the well. No one spoke to her, although a few glanced at her curiously. She thought of Rachel, of Nathan.

She went to the inn. She had not seen it for twenty-five years. It had not changed except that it was more shabby, more decrepit. She had thought to go directly to the barn, but instead she entered the inn. She had no desire to see her parents. She did not even know whether they were alive, and she did not care.

She stood in the doorway, looking about her. Two coarse-looking men sat drinking while two women sat beside them, flirting with them. They looked at Miriam but no one spoke. An old woman stirred something in a pot

173

in the corner. Miriam did not recognize her, but she knew the woman was not her mother.

Then she saw a man seated in a far corner of the room. He looked as old as any man she had ever seen. A covering was thrown over his legs. Miriam looked at his hands. The right one twitched and trembled constantly. The left lay still on his lap, heavy, lifeless. She looked at his face. It was distorted, the left side drooping so that his face appeared to be divided in half. The two sides did not match. A trickle of saliva showed at the side of the slack mouth. His eyes were vacant.

My father, Miriam thought. *My father.* A feeling of revulsion passed through her, so strong that she clenched her teeth against crying out.

The old woman came toward Miriam. "Are you looking for lodging? We don't often get women alone." Her eyes were suspicious.

One of the men said, "She can share my bed." Everyone laughed. He drank his wine and sent Miriam the kind of look she knew so well.

Miriam stared him down and spoke to the old woman. "Yes, I would like to stay. In the loft. Alone." She glanced toward the loft which had been her early refuge.

"You know this place?" The woman sounded surprised.

"Yes. From long ago." Miriam motioned toward her father and asked, "How long has he been like this?"

"Him?" The woman looked at him with contempt. "For more than a year. He can't talk, he can't walk, he can't go to the privy. He soils himself and I have to tend to him. I have to feed him. He's worse off now than he was before when he was drunk all the time. He's no use to me any more. He's no man. A gourd has more life than he does,

174

and a better shape." The others laughed as if they had heard all this before. "But he can't live forever," the old woman said, "and when he's gone, I've got an inn."

"Are you his wife?" Miriam asked.

"Me? His wife? Not likely. He killed one wife."

"What do you mean?"

"His wife is dead, long ago. If you ask me, it was him finally killed her. Hit her too many times."

Miriam felt nothing. Her mother was dead and she could not grieve. "His sons?"

"You knew them, too?" The woman's smile was sly, malicious. "Gone. Left here, all of them, and who could blame them? The oldest is a bad one, always stirring up trouble. They say he's in prison now in Jerusalem. For murder. I hope they keep him there."

Miriam realized that the news had not reached Bethlehem.

"There was a girl," the woman continued. "People say she left when she was young. They say the old man sold her to get rid of her. A fancy harlot she is, they say. Fancy, but a harlot, nonetheless. No one knows where she is. Nor cares."

She might have been talking about strangers. None of her words touched Miriam. The couples at the table were becoming more passionate in their explorations of each other. Miriam's father sat unmoving.

"I would like some soup," Miriam told the old woman. "Bread, too, and water. You can help me take them up to the loft."

She grumbled, but she served Miriam. In the loft Miriam bathed her dusty feet, her hands and face. She ate the soup and bread with a sudden hunger, realizing that she had not eaten much for two days.

When she had finished she stretched out on the straw mat and looked at the sky. It was the same sky, the same small room. But nothing else was the same. She put the knife beside her where she could reach it easily, and she shut her eyes. At once she fell into a sleep so profound that when she awoke she did not know where she was, nor what the day or hour.

She looked out toward the sky, remembering. Night had come while she slept. She heard a creaking on the stair. Old ghosts, old fears stirred in her. She took the knife into her hand, testing its edge. Then a man stood looking down at her, one of the men from downstairs, swaying and leering. She glared at him and showed him her knife. Without speaking, he left her alone.

Miriam was so spent, so without hope or purpose that days and nights passed and she hardly noticed. The old woman grudgingly gave her food and drink. Miriam, careful not to let her see the traveling bag, paid her a gold coin.

And she waited, waited for the strength to do what she was determined she would do. The days of her wasted life passed before her, there in her loft, as she lay waiting. Behind her eyes she saw the scarred, triumphant face of her brother, Jesus Barabbas. Three crosses on a hill. A body placed in a new tomb. The end of hope. The end of life.

***

One morning, waking in her loft, Miriam knew she could delay no longer. She opened her traveling bag and looked at the contents. She wondered what would become of the coins and the jewels, but she did not really care. In the bottom of the bag she found one small, smooth stone. She laid it against her cheek for a moment before she returned it to the bag. Then, taking the bag and her knife, she went to the barn.

It had not changed. The stalls were empty, but they were the same. The feeding box where Jesus had slept was the same, and wisps of hay were scattered in the manger, in the stalls. Spiders had woven elaborate webs which festooned the stalls and shimmered as bits of slanting light fell on them.

Miriam stood beside the manger trying to bring into her mind the picture of the three as they had been, Joseph, Mary, and the baby. And of herself, the child Miriam. But intruding upon her inner sight were three crosses and the face of the man dying on the center one.

Her small reservoir of strength was gone, and she slid to the floor. She sat there seeing nothing, feeling nothing.

She took the knife into her hand. It was sharp. She had kept it so all during the years. With it she had scarred the face of her brother. Now, with it she would end her own life. She knew that nothing waited for her, nothing in this life and nothing in Sheol. Only darkness.

She turned the knife in her hands, wondering how much it would hurt when the steel entered her flesh. *How long will it take me to die?* she wondered. *Will I be thirsty, as Jesus was thirsty?* She had brought no water with her.

She looked at the knife. Light glinted upon it. Her hand was steady. She took a deep breath. Suddenly a shadow

177

fell upon the blade and she looked up. A man stood before her, a stranger. She was startled because she had neither heard nor seen him enter. He was not one of the men from the inn. She did not know him.

He spoke. "Peace be with you, Miriam."

Her heart stopped beating for an instant and she was filled with terror. She could not believe what she heard, what she saw. It was Jesus who called her name. She knew his voice. She saw him standing there, alive.

He spoke again. "Do not be afraid."

She shook her head in disbelief. The knife slipped from her hand. Her terror grew. She had seen him die, seen his body taken down from the cross. She had watched while it was wrapped in a shroud and placed in a garden tomb.

But he was here. This was not a spirit, but a living man. "Miriam," he said again, "look at me. See my hands." He lifted them and held them out. The deep imprints of the nails were there. On his brow she could see the marks of thorns. His eyes knew her.

Miriam collapsed at his feet. Once again she bathed them with her tears. She kissed those wounded feet and wept and could not speak.

He asked her, "Have you a bit of bread and some wine?"

She stood, backed away from him, and, still without speaking, she ran to the inn. The old woman was nowhere in sight and the others had gone. Only Miriam's father sat in his corner and he did not look at her. She seized a basket, placed in it a half-used loaf, a wineskin, and cups, and she hurried back to the barn.

Jesus stood with his hand on the manger, looking down into the empty box. Timidly Miriam offered him the loaf.

178

He took the bread from her and blessed it. Then he broke a piece from the loaf and handed it to her, and another for himself.

He blessed the wine and poured it, handing one cup to Miriam. They ate and drank together there in the room where he had been born.

A spirit cannot eat and drink, Miriam thought. *He was dead. But now he is alive. I do not know how that can be, but he is here.* She thought of the father of the boy whose demon Jesus had banished. "I believe," he had cried. "Help my unbelief."

Jesus said, "Miriam, do you remember that I forgave you all your sins and told you to go and live a new life?"

"Yes, Lord." Miriam hardly recognized her own voice, it was so weak and unsteady.

"That is what you must do now," he told her. "You must forgive all those who have harmed you, just as I have forgiven those who did me harm. I must leave you now. You will not see me again in this life, but I do not leave you without comfort. Speak to me and I will hear you, although you cannot see me. Ask me for what you need, and I will give it to you. Remember to thank my father, for it is from him that all gifts come, through me. Now give me your hand."

She held out her right hand.

"The other hand. The one which was wounded for my sake."

She reached out her left hand to him, that hand which was scarred and puckered and discolored. He took it into both his own and closed his eyes. Miriam felt heat flow into her hand from his. It throbbed with warmth. After a moment he released it.

Miriam looked at her hand. The scars were gone. It was whole. Perfect. She turned it over again and again, touching it, comparing it with her other hand. It was true. He had made it new.

"I have come to make all things new," he said, "and you must witness for me in your new life. Go in peace to love and serve me, for you live in my kingdom."

Before she could answer him he vanished from her sight.

She knelt before the manger where Mary had laid him, the manger which a child once had filled with hay for him to lie upon. She stroked her hand, held it against her cheek, marveled at its perfection.

Has he made the inside of me as new as he has made my hand? she wondered. *Somehow I will learn. For his sake I will find the way to love and serve him as he has told me.*

Miriam touched the cup from which he had drunk. She touched the floor where he had stood. She gathered her new life around her as if it were a robe, and prepared to wear it.

16

At last Miriam knew what she must do with her life, whatever remained of it. There in the barn her weakness was replaced by a new sense of vigor and purpose. She gathered up the rest of the bread and wine, put them with the cups into the basket and took it to the inn. The old woman sat drinking wine.

Without speaking to her, Miriam took her bag up to the loft. She took from it two gold pieces and went down again to face the old woman.

"I can no longer use you here," she said. "Here is pay for what you have done for my father."

The old woman stared at her. "Your father? Then you are the fancy . . . "

"I am Miriam Barabbas." Miriam looked directly at the woman as she spoke. "His daughter."

"So you've come back." The small, spiteful eyes shifted from Miriam to the helpless man in the corner. "Well, you're welcome to him. I've had about all I can take from him anyway. And what's this inn?" She looked around her with scorn. "Not much of a place. Nobody comes here anymore."

Miriam did not answer.

"I suppose you'll be turning it into a fancy brothel. Well, you'll not last long in Bethlehem."

"That is not my plan," Miriam said. "Now you must go."

When the old woman had gone, grumbling, Miriam sat looking at her father. She fought against the thoughts, the pictures which poured into her mind. When she had cleared them all away she said, "Father? *Abba?*"

There was no response. He sat motionless except for the palsied hand in constant motion on his lap.

"That was the hand with which you held mine in the fire," she said, knowing he would not understand. "Look." She held up her hand, smooth and whole. "See? What you did has been undone."

But some things can never be undone, she thought. *Nevertheless, I will make a new start.*

As if she were preparing for guests, Miriam cleaned the inn. She swept, scrubbed, and aired until it was fresh and welcoming. When she had finished, she was weary. Her hands, unused to such work, ached and some of the nails were broken. She had two blisters. But she looked at her hands and laughed.

In the days that followed she tended her father. He never recognized her. He was unaware of anything around him. His only pleasure appeared to be in the taste of the food which she fed him, in the wine she helped him sip.

At first Miriam thought she could not bear to be near him. She had to do everything for him. This was the man who had burned her, who had allowed her to be abused, who had sold her. Her father. She had to bathe him, wash

182

his soiled clothing, tend him as if he were an infant and she the mother.

When she would recoil, upon touching him, she would see her own hand against his flesh. Her hand, perfect as if it had never been burned. Then she was able to think of him as an infant and of herself as new. Or she would think of him as a stranger who was dependent upon her for his life. This ruined man seemed oddly detached from her, and she from him.

One day she had a visitor. Mary of Magdala came to the inn alone. The two women looked at each other. Again Miriam was struck by their resemblance to each other. Again she felt that she might be seeing her own daughter.

"You are welcome here," she told her visitor. "I am happy to see you again. How did you find me?"

"The mother of Jesus thought you might come here."

She knew, Miriam thought.

Mary of Magdala looked at the man in the corner. "Your father?"

"Yes."

"I know much of your story." She spoke without judgment. "Our friend has told me much about you. About what you did for the three of them when her son was born and how you suffered for it."

Miriam nodded but did not speak.

Mary came to her and took both Miriam's hands in her own, examining them. "Was not one of your hands burned for his sake?"

"Yes." Miriam was able to say the word calmly, with no return of the burning rage which had been part of her for so long.

"Which one?"

Miriam raised her left hand toward Mary.

"But it is perfect." Her gaze was steady, clear. "He has been here, then? You have seen him?"

"Yes." Miriam was filled with joy. Here was someone with whom she could talk about the mystery of his return, the wonder of her own healing.

"He healed your hand?" Mary Magdalene asked. "After his death?"

"Yes. Out in the barn where he was born. He came to me just as I was going to . . . "

"To?"

"I had decided not to go on living. But he came, and I am alive. Truly alive."

"I understand. He healed me, too," Mary said. "That was before his death. What he did for me cannot be seen with the eyes, for it was nothing visible which he healed. It was an inner cleansing."

Miriam did not tell of her own inner cleansing. *Perhaps she knows*, she thought.

"Do you believe in demons?" Mary asked Miriam.

"Yes." Miriam did not have to think before answering for she had seen the boy possessed by demons. She had watched him writhe and foam and struggle against the evil which inhabited him. And she had watched and listened when Jesus commanded the demons to leave him. She had seen them go. "Oh yes, I believe in demons," she said to Mary.

"I was possessed by demons," Mary of Magdala told Miriam. "All my life they lived in me. There were seven and I knew them all. I named them secretly and called them by their names, begging them to leave me."

Miriam watched as she looked into past years, her

luminous eyes fixed on another time. She was very lovely, as lovely as Miriam herself had been at twenty, but with a difference, for she was inhabited by love.

"I never knew," Mary said, "when they would seize me and make me do the things I most wished not to do. They ruled my life. I was called 'The Mad One.' All of Magdala knew. My parents were ashamed of me. My father's wealth could not give him a healthy, docile daughter. My mother wept much and wrung her hands. I could never please my parents. I would beg my demons to leave me, but they would not."

Miriam wondered what they had been like, the demons which had ruled this woman. Now sunlight fell upon her hair touching it with flame. Her voice was musical and soft as she spoke out of her memories.

"I had fine clothing, jewels, all the delicacies which my father's money could buy. But I had no real life of my own. What I wished to do I could not do, and the things I did not wish to do, I did. The demons governed my hands and feet, my mouth, my entire body. Only sometimes, when they seemed to be resting, I could feel, deep within myself like a little flame, the flicker of the self I wished to be."

Miriam leaned toward her. "I know. I know."

"Then one day," Mary said, "Jesus came to Magdala. He was on his way somewhere else, it does not matter where. I saw him. It was one of those moments when my demons were resting and my small flame burned weakly. My spirit's flame.

"We met on the road outside town and he looked at me. Our eyes met and I knew in that instant that he could help me. He alone recognized me, knew me. I think I cried

185

out to him, although it may have been only my heart that cried. *Save me,* I begged him. *Save me.*"

Again Miriam thought of the boy writhing on the ground and of the way Jesus had looked when he commanded the evil spirits to leave him.

Mary said, "I felt my demons leave me. I vomited them out with all my strength, all my consciousness. I was alone in the dark for a long time, it seemed to me. Then Jesus was speaking my name, my hands were in his and I was ... Mary. He named me. He gave me back to myself. He made me new."

Miriam had heard him say, *I have come to make all things new.*

"The demons have not returned," Mary said, "and I know they never will. That was my healing. And that day I offered him my life, for all time."

Miriam could see that she was whole. Radiance glowed from within her. "Have you seen him too? Since his death?" she asked.

"Yes, I have seen him. I was the first to see him. The first."

"Will you tell me?"

"I did not sleep at all the night after he died."

Miriam had not slept either.

"On the sabbath we were all too numb to think or speak, his mother and the others and I. It was as if something had died within each of us when he died.

"On the day after the sabbath I went alone to the tomb to begin the preparation of his body. Somehow I needed to be alone. I could not have talked to anyone. It was still dark. I remember thinking that it might never be light again, without him.

186

"When I approached the tomb I saw that the great stone had been rolled away. It lay apart from the tomb. I was frightened, but I went to look inside." She was silent and Miriam felt that she was lost in memory.

"Then?" Miriam asked.

"The tomb was empty. I was sure that someone had stolen his body. I did not know what to do. In a panic I ran to tell Simon Peter and John. They hurried back with me to look. His body was not there, but the grave cloths were. It was too much to bear, I thought. First they killed him and then they took his body away from us before we could anoint and prepare it.

"The men went away again. I stayed outside the tomb and I could not stop crying. After a while, just to see once more the place where his body had lain, I looked inside again. I do not expect you to believe what I saw then, but I will tell you."

"I will believe whatever you tell me," Miriam assured her. "I also have seen things too strange to be believed."

"At the head and foot of the place where he had lain were . . . I cannot call them men, for although they were like men, they were not. They were beings all white and shining. And they had great wings which circled and surrounded them with light. I had to look away from their brightness."

Miriam thought of the Messenger who had come to her that night in her loft, in a dream.

"They did not speak to me in words," Mary said, "but I understood them. They asked me, *Why are you weeping?*

"I did not answer them in words, but inside my mind I told them, *Because they have taken away my Lord and I do not know where they have laid him.*

187

"Then I knew that they wanted me to go outside the tomb. I felt bathed in the light which issued from them, and all the while I thought I must surely be dreaming."

"Oh I know, I know," Miriam said.

"And then, outside in the garden I saw a man, a stranger. I thought he must be the gardener come to tend the flowers before the heat of the day.

"He, too, asked me why I was weeping. I thought that perhaps for some reason he was the one who had taken away the body of Jesus. Or perhaps he knew who had. I asked him, 'Sir, if you have carried him away, tell me where you have laid him, and I will take him away.' I remember that as I said it I wondered how I could do it alone, even if I were to find him.

"Then he said my name. *Mary.* It was his voice, his own voice, and all at once I knew him. The world was bright again. He was alive."

Miriam's heart began to race. She had felt the same way when she saw him in the barn.

"He told me not to delay him but to go and tell the others. Oh Miriam, he was himself, as he had been, only even more himself. I cannot explain it. He did not tell me where he had been in those days since his death. But it was he. I knew him."

"Yes. I know."

Mary said quietly, "I am not sure the others believed me when I told them. Later they did, for they saw him too. But at first they did not believe me."

"I believe you," Miriam said. "He came to me, too, out in the barn. He healed me. Sometimes I cannot grasp how it can possibly be so." She looked at her hand, unblemished and clean. "But I know it is true."

188

"Yes," Mary of Magdala said, "it is true. He died and he rose from death." She sighed. Then she asked Miriam, "What will you do now?"

"I am not sure. I only know that in some way I must serve him." She glanced at her father. "I must care for my father. I know that. And somehow I must learn to forgive him for all he did to me. What else I must do, I do not know yet."

Mary looked at her thoughtfully. "I wonder," she said, "whether you might be the one to help."

"What do you mean?"

"I know a child," Mary said, "a girl who has been cruelly treated. She has no one. She is with a friend of mine just now. But I believe you might be the one to help her most. You will recognize her suffering because of your own. May I bring her to you to care for, at least for a time?"

"I know nothing about children," Miriam protested.

"You were just such a child," Mary reminded her. "You will know what to do for her. Let me bring her to you."

"What is her name? How old is she?" Miriam tried to put time between the request and her answer.

"She is eight years old. Her name is Sara." Mary paused before she added, "Since she was harmed she has not spoken."

Miriam thought of that silent child in the loft, the child slowly turning to ice, to stone. "Yes, bring her to me," she said. "Bring her here to me."

17

"Come, Sara. I'll show you how we feed Abba." Although Sara never spoke, Miriam continued to talk to her as though she might speak at any moment.

From the day she was brought to the inn Sara touched a part of Miriam which had not been touched since she had responded to that wretched small girl in Egypt long ago. Sara was thin, pale, silent. But Miriam thought that she saw a wary response deep in the child's eyes. Miriam had bathed the fragile, unresisting body, had combed the tangled black hair and had dressed the child in new clothing: a flaxen robe with a scarlet sash and a band of scarlet on the head shawl. Miriam wondered whether the new clothes might cheer the little girl.

Sara responded only with that oblique look. But Miriam was sure that one day the girl would speak. Meanwhile she talked to her as she would talk to any adult. Miriam had almost forgotten what it was like to be a child. She had had no real childhood of her own. She hoped that she might be able to provide Sara with one.

"See," she said to the girl as she dipped a small bit of gruel from the clay pot, "we give Abba only a small bit at a time. It is hard for him to swallow." She fed her

191

father the spoonful. He swallowed it and opened his mouth for more.

Miriam glanced at Sara. "You see? He likes it. He opens his mouth like a baby bird. Will you feed him?"

But the child cowered behind Miriam. Miriam felt her trembling. "Not today? Never mind. Some day, maybe."

Wherever Miriam went Sara followed, a small shadow. She clutched a rag doll and was never parted from it, even when she slept.

On the day Miriam had put Sara's new robe on her, she had also dressed the doll in a robe like Sara's. Sara had almost smiled. Miriam could see a relaxing of the tight mouth, a lifting of the darkness in the dark eyes.

But days, weeks passed, and the child remained mute. She watched Miriam feed her father but she never approached him. Miriam could sense her fear. She had known just such fear herself. She understood it well.

Sara slept beside Miriam on a mat in the loft. Sometimes Miriam watched her as she slept, wondering what memories were stored up in that small head, what pain clouded her dreams. When she moaned or cried in her sleep Miriam held her, soothed her, murmured to her even though she did not fully waken.

In the deep of a night several weeks after the child had come to the inn, Miriam was awakened by a pounding at the door. She looked at Sara. The girl slept deeply. Miriam hurried down the steps and stood at the closed door.

"What is it? Who is there?"

"Miriam, let me in. Someone is in trouble."

Miriam recognized the voice. It was the wife of Rachel's

192

youngest son. She unbarred the door. "Who is in trouble?" she asked the young woman.

"We don't know him. We've never seen him. Someone called to us and when we went, this stranger had collapsed outside our house. Can we bring him to you? We have no room."

Those words chimed in Miriam's mind, an echo from the dark past. Once there had been no room for three others here, in this very place.

"Yes. Have your husband bring him here."

Miriam hastily prepared a mat in the corner of the inn near the place where her father slept. They laid the stranger there.

"I do not think he is wounded," Miriam's neighbor told her. "I think he has fever. And see how thin he is."

"Yes." Miriam felt the stranger's head. "He is burning."

The stranger opened his eyes and looked at her. "Water?" he whispered.

She brought him water. When he had sipped it he lay back with a deep sigh and slept again.

Miriam looked down at him, wondering what his story might be. Suddenly she was conscious of a presence near her. Sara, holding her doll, stood beside her, her eyes frightened.

"It's all right," Miriam said. "You don't have to be afraid. It's just someone who is sick, who needs our help. See? He is sleeping." She looked at her father and she said to Sara, "Abba is sleeping too. Now we'll go back upstairs."

Sara lay down near Miriam. Miriam bent and kissed

the rag doll. "Good night," she said. "Sweet dreams." She looked at Sara, a question in her eyes.

Sara patted her own cheek. Miriam bent and kissed her. "Good night, Sara. Sweet dreams."

It's the first step, Miriam thought. *She let me kiss her. Soon she'll speak to me. I know it.*

But time passed and Sara did not speak. Word spread in the village that Miriam had taken a sick stranger into the inn and before long the inn had become a sort of hospice where the sick and needy were cared for.

So this is to be my function, Miriam thought. *This is what I am to do with my life. So be it.*

Miriam engaged two young men from the village to help with the lifting and carrying. And she began to wonder how long her gold would last.

One day she had visitors. Mary of Magdala came with two of the men who had been close friends of Jesus: Peter and John. Miriam was pleased to see them. The villagers, except for the family of Rachel, did not come near her. Her only company was a helpless father, a speechless child, and her sick.

Now here were people who had known and loved Jesus. She wanted to hear them talk about him. She was famished for words about him, for news of his mother.

"First, before we talk," Mary said, "let us eat and drink together in his name, as he told his friends to do."

Remembering her own experience with him the day he came to her in the barn, Miriam brought bread and wine. Peter blessed them and Miriam felt the presence of Jesus among them as they shared the meal in his memory. *He is with us,* she thought, and looking at the faces of the others, she knew that they, too, felt his presence.

194

"Now," Peter said, "let us teach you a prayer which he taught us. It may help you when you feel alone."

Sara watched, wide-eyed, as Miriam sat with her friends. Miriam drew her close, holding her so that she would not be afraid.

"Yes," Miriam said. "Teach us how to pray. I have never known how. Listen now, Sara. Peter is going to teach us something we will learn together, you and I."

The child leaned against Miriam, embracing her doll as Miriam embraced her.

She trusts me. Miriam was filled with quiet joy at the weight of the small body against her own.

Peter smiled at the child as he spoke. "Here is the prayer that our friend Jesus told us to use. Now listen carefully."

As Miriam listened it was as if she heard the voice of Jesus once again. Peter's voice, vibrant but quiet, spoke words which she knew had first come from the mouth of Jesus, the one who had saved her life.

"Father in Heaven," Peter prayed, "whose Name is holy, may the Kingdom come. May earth, like Heaven, fulfill your will."

The Kingdom, Miriam thought. *There it is again, that Kingdom which is not of this world.*

"Give us the bread we need," Peter continued. "Forgive us as we forgive those who have wronged us."

I try, Miriam thought, almost pleading. *I try, but I still have not forgiven my father, my brother, all those who harmed me.*

"Do not test us in Tribulation, but protect us from the Evil One."

I have seen the Evil One, Miriam thought. *I have seen his face on the faces of men. We all need to be delivered.*

"This is the prayer as he taught it to us," Peter said. "We use it each day. And the ritual meal, too, we use when we gather together. We eat and drink in memory of him."

Mary of Magdala told Miriam, "I have brought some gold for you to use here in your work. I want to help, for I know you are doing it in his name."

Gratefully Miriam accepted the coins.

"And I have brought this for Sara." Mary slipped a necklace of bright beads over the child's head. "See how pretty it looks."

But Sara hid behind Miriam.

When they had all left, Miriam said to Sara, "It is time to feed Abba. Will you help me today?"

Sara did not answer, but she stood nearby while Miriam fed her father his gruel and wine. Sara seemed fascinated by the hand which trembled on his lap. She watched it silently.

Forgive, forgive, forgive. The words rang in Miriam's head as she fed this man, her enemy, her abuser. *When will I ever be able to forgive him?* She closed her eyes, her body tense with old hates.

She felt a tug at her sleeve. "Imma, Abba is crying."

Miriam looked down at Sara, unable to believe what she had heard. *She called me Imma. Mother.* She stared at the child.

Impatiently the girl said again, "Abba is crying."

Miriam looked away from Sara toward her father. The old man's eyes were fixed on Sara and tears ran down his face. With his trembling hand he reached toward her.

196

The girl took the palsied hand in her own and laid it against her cheek. "Poor Abba," she said. "Don't cry. Sara will feed you." Sara laid her doll down and, taking the spoon from Miriam, she began feeding the old man, crooning to him as if he were a doll or a baby.

Looking up at Miriam over her shoulder Sara asked, "Why is Abba crying?"

Miriam shook her head, unable to answer.

"Why?" Sara persisted. "Does he feel bad? Does his hand hurt? It shakes all the time. Does it hurt him?"

"I don't think so," Miriam said.

"Then why does he cry? Is he unhappy?"

"Yes. I think he must be unhappy." *How could he not be unhappy?* Miriam thought.

"Can we make him happy?" Sara asked.

"I think it makes him happy when you feed him," Miriam told her.

Sara fed him the rest of the gruel. Then she picked up her doll and sat beside the old man until he fell asleep. Miriam watched them, bewildered by the sudden change in Sara.

As if she felt Miriam's eyes watching her, Sara went to her. "You are not my imma, are you?" she asked.

"No."

"I wish you were."

"We could pretend that I am," Miriam said.

Sara's eyes held dark secrets. She put her hand into Miriam's and asked, "Do you wish you were my imma?"

"Yes."

"Then you are."

"All right." Miriam asked seriously, "Are you sure?"

"Yes. And Abba can be my abba?"

197

"What about your own Imma? Your own Abba?" Miriam asked.

The panic returned to Sara's eyes and she looked away without speaking.

Miriam said gently, "It's all right. You don't have to tell me."

Sara looked at her for a long moment before she said, "My abba hurt me. Your abba won't hurt me. Will he?"

Miriam fought against tears. "No. He won't hurt you," she assured Sara.

"So he can be my abba. I'll feed him and sing to him and he won't cry any more."

"Good." Miriam embraced the child.

"Were you his little girl?" Sara asked.

"Yes." Miriam felt as if each word she spoke about her father was a rough stone which tore her throat and mouth as she said it.

"Now you're a lady, so I'll be his little girl." Sara glanced at the sleeping man. "When he wakes up I'll sing to him."

Miriam looked at the man whose life was nearing its close, at the child whose life, like her own, had begun with abuse; the child now in her care. *Father in Heaven,* she prayed silently, *may earth, like Heaven, fulfill your will. Forgive me, for I do not know how to forgive.* The words of the prayer deserted her. Clenching her hands so that the nails bit into her palms she prayed blindly, *Help me. Oh help me.*

18

"Imma," Sara tugged at Miriam's hand, "that lady is here."

Miriam looked up to see Mary, the mother of Jesus, standing in the doorway. John was beside her. She hurried to greet them.

"My dear child," Mary said, embracing her.

I will always be a child to her, Miriam thought.

"We have come to see how things are with you." John looked about him at the people lying on pallets on the floor of the inn.

Miriam asked him, "Are you looking for someone?"

John said, "I look for him. For Jesus. He said he would come again, and I look for him in everyone I meet. Sometimes I think I see him."

Miriam looked at Mary, feasting on the sight of her face. It was serene and strong although pain lines marked the eyes and mouth. "I am so glad you have come," Miriam said.

"I have brought you something." Mary took from John a small metal chest, beautifully incised, and she offered it to Miriam.

Miriam recognized the box. She began to protest.

Mary said, "The spices were used as the magi said they would be used. Now you are to use the gold for your ministry to these least ones." She looked at the sick who lay all around her.

Miriam took the heavy box. "Would the magi have traveled so far and brought such gifts if they had known how he was to die?" she asked Mary.

"Perhaps they had learned from their stars that death could not hold him," Mary answered. "Yes, I believe they were destined to bring their gifts."

Sara pulled at Miriam's sleeve. "Look." She pointed to the doorway. Miriam saw a man clinging to the doorpost, swaying as if he could hardly stand.

"Help me," she said to the two men who served her. When they touched his back the man groaned. They laid him face down on a pallet and she went to him. Mary and John followed. Miriam examined the deep wound which she found in his back. It had festered and livid streaks radiated from it.

"This one is far gone," one of the young men said.

Miriam agreed. "But we can try to make him comfortable." She had not looked at the man's face, only at his wound. After she had bathed it and they turned him over she looked at his face. It was drawn with pain, fevered and distorted. His beard was matted with sweat.

Then Miriam saw the scar which ran from the corner of his left eye across to the nose. She gasped and dropped the cloth with which she had bathed him. She stood frozen.

"Imma?" Sara looked up into Miriam's face.

Miriam put her hand on the child's head, hoping Sara would not feel it tremble. "It's all right."

200

Sara looked down at the injured man whose glazed eyes stared at her, unseeing. Crowding closer to Miriam she said, in a voice barely audible, "That's my Abba. He hurt me." Her large eyes grew dark with fear and Miriam felt her quivering. "I don't like him."

Why am I not surprised? Miriam asked herself. *Why does nothing about this man surprise me?*

She looked at Mary. Together they looked down at Jesus Barabbas. The Enemy. Miriam felt the old rage flare with a fire strong enough to consume her. This man was the very embodiment of Evil.

He looked up at her, lips cracked and bleeding with fever. In a voice which was scarcely human he said, "I am thirsty."

Miriam thought of another whose eyes were full of agony, whose lips were cracked with his last fever. He had said the same words.

She looked at Mary, whose eyes were closed. *She's praying,* Miriam thought. She looked down at the child beside her, the child she had come to love. The child who shared her own heritage, who shared her pain, inflicted by this same man. And she rejoiced with a fierce, wild knowledge.

She faced her lifelong enemy. She could withhold water from him. She could watch him die slowly as the other Jesus had died. How often she had longed for this moment. How often she had plotted his death as she lay in her loft.

Again he looked at her and croaked in that desperate voice, "Water."

Miriam knew that he did not recognize her. How had he come to this place? Was he like a wounded beast crawl-

ing back to its lair to die? As she stared at him the flood
of the past nearly drowned her.

Without a glance at Mary, John, or Sara, Miriam left
the inn. She ran to the barn and stood beside the feeding
trough, heart pounding, breath labored as if she had run
for miles. *It is too much,* she thought. *I cannot help him.
It is too much to ask.*

Unable to pray or even to think, Miriam stood, hands
clenched, the fire of her old anger flaming within her. She
plunged her hands deep into the pocket of her gown. One
hand touched an object which she always carried with
her. A small, smooth stone. As if it burned her, Miriam
withdrew her hand from it. She sank to her knees beside
the feeding trough.

Soon Mary stood beside her. Miriam looked up at her.
"You recognized him?"

"Yes. Your brother. Jesus Barabbas."

"I cannot forgive him." Miriam's voice shook. "I hate
him for what he did to me, to Sara. To you. How can I
forgive him? It is too much to ask. Too much." She
reached into her pocket for the smooth stone and laid it
against her cheek, savoring its coolness.

"What is that?" Mary asked her.

Miriam showed it to her.

"A stone. Is it a keepsake then?"

Miriam shuddered.

"I know the story." Mary's voice was calm. "It is a stone
which no one cast?"

Miriam looked up at her, pleading in her eyes. "I cannot. I cannot."

Mary said, "I understand your feeling. I truly understand." She laid her hand against the manger, stroking
202

the rough wood. "Do you remember?" she asked Miriam.

"Of course." Miriam remembered everything.

A radiant, shining being which encircled her with wings of light.

Her own small self, listening to stars which sang.

A baby's fingers curling around her own.

Everything which had happened in this barn.

The young Miriam, her body cruelly abused.

The dead boy babies.

All the men she had cheated.

A leper cleansed.

A young boy, cleansed of his demon, calling her beautiful.

A young girl, once dead, restored to life.

A hand on her head and a voice whose kindness released her tears, melting the inner core of stone and ice which had imprisoned her for so long.

That same voice saying, "Go in peace. Your sins are forgiven you."

And, in this very place, her hand made whole, her life redeemed.

Rocking back and forth there beside his cradle Miriam wept.

Mary said, "Shall we pray together? Or, if you cannot, stay beside me for a moment."

Still Miriam wept.

Mary said, "Father in Heaven whose Name is holy, may the Kingdom come."

Miriam listened, but could not speak. Mary's voice drifted past her as she tried to stop her tears. Then she heard the words, "Forgive us as we forgive those who have wronged us."

When Mary's voice was silent Miriam said, "I do not understand any of it. I am too weak to be able to do what he said. I do not understand at all."

Mary smiled and drew her to her feet. "It is not necessary to understand," she said. "Only believe and trust. And do the best you can. He will help you."

Together Mary and Miriam went back to the inn. Sara ran to Miriam. "Your Abba is crying. Shall I feed him? Shall I sing to him?"

Miriam took her hand. "Let us see what he needs." They went to Miriam's father. Tears ran down his cheeks and he reached his trembling hand toward Sara. She cradled it in her own small hands. "Don't cry, Abba," she said. "Sara is here. Shall I sing to you?" Not waiting for the answer which she knew would not come, she began to sing to him.

Miriam turned to look at her brother.

Sara stopped singing and clutched her hand. "Don't go to him," she begged. "He will hurt us."

Gently Miriam disengaged the small hand from her own. "He will not hurt us any more," she told the child. "He is too sick. Now we must take care of him. Will you help me?"

But Sara shook her head. Miriam saw that she trembled with the old fear. "Never mind," she said. "You stay with Abba. He needs you."

Sara took the old man's hand and began to sing to him again.

Miriam turned toward Mary and John. Looking at Mary as if to beg for her help, Miriam went to her brother. Kneeling beside him she raised his head and supported him as she gave him a drink of cool water.

204

CHRISTIAN HERALD ASSOCIATION AND ITS MINISTRIES

CHRISTIAN HERALD ASSOCIATION, founded in 1878, publishes The Christian Herald Magazine, one of the leading interdenominational religious monthlies in America. Through its wide circulation, it brings inspiring articles and the latest news of religious developments to many families. From the magazine's pages came the initiative for CHRISTIAN HERALD CHILDREN and THE BOWERY MISSION, two individually supported not-for-profit corporations.

CHRISTIAN HERALD CHILDREN, established in 1894, is the name for a unique and dynamic ministry to disadvantaged children, offering hope and opportunities which would not otherwise be available for reasons of poverty and neglect. The goal is to develop each child's potential and to demonstrate Christian compassion and understanding to children in need.

Mont Lawn is a permanent camp located in Bushkill, Pennsylvania. It is the focal point of a ministry which provides a healthful "vacation with a purpose" to children who without it would be confined to the streets of the city. Up to 1000 children between the age of 7 and 11 come to Mont Lawn each year.

Christian Herald Children maintains year-round contact with children by means of a *City Youth Ministry*. Central to its philosophy is the belief that only through sustained relationships and demonstrated concern can individual lives be truly enriched. Special emphasis is on individual guidance, spiritual and family counseling and tutoring. This follow-up ministry to inner-city children culminates for many in financial assistance toward higher education and career counseling.

THE BOWERY MISSION, located at 227 Bowery, New York City, has since 1879 been reaching out to the lost men on the Bowery, offering them what could be their last chance to rebuild their lives. Every man is fed, clothed and ministered to. Countless numbers have entered the 90-day residential rehabilitation program at the Bowery Mission. A concentrated ministry of counseling, medical care, nutrition therapy, Bible study and Gospel services awakens a man to spiritual renewal within himself.

These ministries are supported solely by the voluntary contributions of individuals and by legacies and bequests. Contributions are tax deductible. Checks should be made out either to CHRISTIAN HERALD CHILDREN or to THE BOWERY MISSION.

Administrative Office: 40 Overlook Drive, Chappaqua, New York 10514
Telephone: (914) 769-9000